Stash Envy

And Other Quilting
Confessions and Adventures

Lisa Boyer

Good Books

Intercourse, PA 17534
800/762-7171
www.GoodBks.com

Cover and Illustrations by Cheryl Benner
Design by Dawn J. Ranck

STASH ENVY
Copyright © 2005 by Good Books, Intercourse, PA 17534
International Standard Book Number: 1-56148-503-9
Library of Congress Catalog Card Number: 2005021821

Library of Congress Cataloging-in-Publication Data
Boyer, Lisa.
Stash envy and other quilting confessions and adventures / Lisa Boyer.
    p. cm.
ISBN 1-56148-503-9 (pbk.)
1. Quilting. 2. Quilts. I. Title.
TT835.B63525 2005
746.46--dc22   2005021821

Table
of Contents

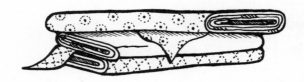

Quilt,
Interrupted

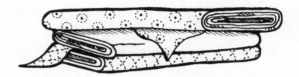

Ah! Quilt Day has finally arrived! I clear the breakfast dishes, pour myself a cup of tea, and walk up the long flight of stairs that leads to my sewing room. On my way, I reflect upon my week and how I've earned this day. Thursday, I did the laundry. Friday, I cleaned the house. Saturday was grocery day, and on Sunday I caught up on my correspondence and paid the bills. My laundry is done, my house is clean, my fridge is stocked. I am to ready enjoy a well-earned day of quilt-making!

In my sewing room, my stack of spring-green, jelly-bean pink, and butter-yellow fabric eyes me suspiciously. These fabrics fear the sharp new blade of my rotary cutter. Ah, tremble in fear, little fabrics, for you shall shortly be re-shaped into strips and forced to do my bidding. I am Quilting Queen of the World, and I proclaim today to be Quilt Day and . . . .

"Brrrrring." Uh-oh . . . the phone. The phone isn't supposed to ring. It's not on the Royal Schedule. How can this happen on Quilt Day?

"Brrrrrring! Brrrrrrring!"

"Hello? Oh . . . a potluck tonight? Eight dozen cupcakes? Alright, I'll be there." Sigh . . .

Okay, back to my fabrics. I won't think about the cupcakes now; I'll think about them later. I wonder if I have any cake mix. Kids won't notice if the cupcakes aren't from scratch. I wonder what flavor I should make. Hey, wait a minute. I'm thinking about cupcakes. I need to think about this fabric. Let me see, what size do I cut these strips?

"Honey?" My husband's voice drifts up the stairs. "Do you know where the pfluumpkerp is?"

Hmmm. I know he didn't really say "pfluumpkerp," but that's what it sounded like. What rhymes with pfluumpkerp? Nothing that I can think of. But if I yell "Whaaaat?" back down the stairs, he'll only say "Huuhhhh?" and that will snowball into an veritable avalanche of "Whats?" and "Huh's?" Resigned to my fate, I pry my unwilling fingers off my rotary cutter and go downstairs to help him find his elusive pfluumpkerp. From past experience, I know that when my husband can't find something, he usually needs help with how to work it, too. Putting it away when he's finished is also a problem.

An hour later I return. My tea is cold, but I'm not

going back downstairs to heat it. I'm going to cut this fabric. Let me see . . . how wide were those strips?

Suddenly, a soft and furry object brushes my ankles. "Meow?" my cat asks. Not now! I think. There's food in your bowl. It's your favorite: Tender Scrambled Fish Cubes. Yummy! Unfazed, my cat looks up at me with wide green eyes full of love and devotion. "Meow . . . prrrrrt?" he asks, beseechingly. Oh please! Just give me a few minutes. Let me cut just one strip.

The cat jumps up onto my fabric and presses his forehead against my cutting-arm elbow. Back downstairs I go. At least I'll be able to reheat my tea and thaw something for dinner. Uh-oh, where's all this water on the kitchen floor coming from?

Two hours later, I return to my fabric. Miraculously, I am able to cut five strips before the phone rings again, the cat runs out of fish parts, and my husband misplaces his blirkenbat. Between these amusing distractions, I make lunch, clean up the dishes, and open a newly arrived batch of mail. By three o'clock I cautiously climb the stairs, determined to sew my five hard-won fabric strips together. I sew one, two, three strips together. Excitedly, I check the instructions to see what the next step is. It's then that I notice that I should have sewn the yellow strip in the middle, not on the left side. No problem, I think; where's my seam ripper?

At that moment, my son walks into my sewing room, just home from school. His shoulders are hunched, his brow is furrowed, and he looks like his world has collapsed. He plops himself down in my sewing chair. With downcast eyes, he stares at the floor. "I had a bad day," he says. "This girl said . . . ."

The Queen lays down her rotary-cutter scepter and quietly abdicates for today. Long Live the Queen of Quilting. She'll have to, if she ever wants to finish a quilt.

An Open Letter to the Worldwide Quilt Judging Organization

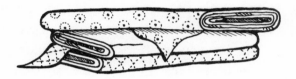

My Dear Esteemed Quilt Judges:

I have long felt that some changes are needed in the OFFICIAL WORLD QUILT JUDGING MANUAL. Since having nominated and appointed myself head representative of the Worldwide Dorky Homemade Quilt Association, I, Lisa Boyer, am hereby forwarding recommendations directly to you. I hope you will carefully consider these insightful changes, as I believe that they will help to create a kinder, gentler, more appreciative atmosphere for all the unfortunate quilts of the world.

Many admirable attributes of the quilt art form have been overlooked and undervalued for far too long. I address this problem here. Toward this purpose, I am proposing that the following point system be used in place of that old point system you've been torturing us with for over a century. (Honestly, aren't you sick of straight seams and perfect stitches by now? Have you no compassion for pitiful quilts?) I submit here an entirely new system of scoring, with the following criteria:

1. (5 points) **Effective Use of Quilt Lumps.** Lumps may be of fabric or batting origin. Misplaced-quilting-tool lumps are disqualified, as are small rodents and/or household-pet lumps. Donuts and other food-stuffs may be awarded lump points, if accessible and edible. Points are awarded for the most effective design flow around the lump(s); in other words, lumps must look accidental and natural and must appear in the worst position imaginable. Quilt lumps inadvertently created in the bull's-eye center of a quilt are awarded bonus embarrassment points.

2. (Up to 20 points) **Color Bravery.** Imagination is finally rewarded in this category. Point increments are awarded as follows:

   a. Inspire a judge to laugh at color choices. Chortles, giggles, and sighs do not receive full credit: 5 points.

   b. Cause a judge to shake his/her head in abject bewilderment: 10 points.

   c. Make a judge wince and develop a sudden headache: 15 points.

    d. Force a judge to shield his/her eyes in order to avoid permanent retinal damage: 20 points.

3. (20 points) **Creative Seam Engineering.** Anyone can make a *straight* seam. Well, almost anyone. Okay, no one that I know personally. But straight seams are so unimaginative! This category rewards the "adventurous seam"—the seam that likes to take its time to fully explore the geography and lump-ography of the quilt. Full points are given for one complete seam that manages to travel 90 degrees or more from its original intended course. Puckers are awarded bonus points.

4. (20 points) **Inventive Placement of Thread-Ball Snarls.** (No fair disguising them to look like something the cat left behind.) Points are awarded based on size and utter entanglement of snarl ball.

5. (10 points) **Effective Use of Ugly Fabric.** Self-explanatory. Full points are awarded for the bravest use of the most horrible, eye-offending fabric imaginable. Bonus points are awarded to the quilter who can take a pretty fabric and make it feel sorry that it ever existed.

6. (5 points) **Most Mysterious Theme.** If you can actually figure out the theme of a quilt, it isn't all that intriguing, is it?

a. Zero points are awarded for discernible themes.

b. A theme that exists solely in the mind of the quiltmaker receives low points. However, if same entrant attempts to explain his/her quilt theme in fancy art words, all points earned are definitely subtracted.

c. A blob quilt, especially if the blobs are not recognizable as earthly objects, shall receive high marks in this category. (Blobs with eyeballs score slightly lower, as anyone can appliqué roadkill.)

Note: Mysteriously themed quilts that have scored historic highs in this category have included: "A Study of Gum Blobs in the Parking Lot" and "Stuff I Saw Under Anesthesia While Having My Gall Bladder Removed."

7. (10 points) **Desperate Last-Minute Quilt Show Additions.** A hot-glued binding is classic in this category. Also rewarded: partial machine quilting (especially if the safety pins are left in), and imaginative paper excuses pinned to quilt. "I would have finished this in time for the quilt show, but my hamster got sick," is a pretty good one. I'd forgive her.

8. (10 Points) **Sincerity.** Difficult to describe a standard for this one. It's more of a gut feeling. How

cuddly is the quilt? Does the quilt make you want to curl up with it, perhaps with a good book? Does it make you think of Grandma's house? Would you wrap your child in it? If this quilt were a person, would it look at you with really big eyes and a grateful smile? If so, full points.

In conclusion, I would like to say, with all due respect to your organization, that these changes are long overdue. The Quilting World awaits your bold and decisive action. I humbly suggest that you implement my recommended point system before May 5th, because I have a quilt show I got tricked into entering and I would finally like to win something for once.

Please?

Sincerely,
Lisa G. Boyer, Dorky Homemade Quiltmaker

Good Ol' "Alice What's-Her-Name"

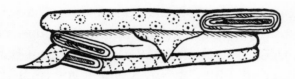

I'll never forget my first time. I had just walked into a guild Christmas-dinner party, and not knowing anyone, I sat down in one of the last remaining chairs in the auditorium. I was new to the area, so I was anxious to make new friends. As the speaker began the program, she urged us to introduce ourselves to the person sitting directly across from us. I looked across the table and extended my hand to the pleasant-looking woman sitting there. "Hi, I'm Lisa Boyer," I said. "Hello," she replied, my name is Judy Mathieson."

"AAAAGGH! Judy MATHIESON!" I yelped, upsetting my water glass into my gift basket of pillow mints. "I HAVE ALL YOUR BOOKS! OH, MY GOSH! I LOVE YOUR QUILTS! Your 'Nautical Stars' quilt is one of the best quilts ever made! I can't believe it! AND HERE YOU ARE, SITTING RIGHT

ACROSS THE TABLE FROM ME!! How did you . . .
are you . . . I CAN'T BELIEVE IT'S REALLY YOU!"

Poor Judy. I'm sure I looked quite normal when I
walked in; how could she know that I would turn into a
rabid lunatic at the mere mention of her name? I think,
after a few minutes of this, she might have said,
"Shhhhh," but otherwise, she just smiled. I don't
remember much of the rest of the evening, but I do
remember trying unsuccessfully not to stare at her while
she ate her vegetables. For the record, Judy Mathieson
eats her peas just like everyone else, just so you know.

I'm sorry; I just can't help it. I am completely star-
struck by famous quilters. The funny thing is that I'm
not all that impressed by TV or movie stars. As a matter of fact, I eat lunch next to Harrison Ford quite fre-
quently at my favorite Japanese restaurant. Well, yes,
it's actually only a *poster* of Harrison Ford, but I figure
it's good practice for remaining calm for when I eventually do meet him for real.

After a year of practicing with Harrison Ford, I
signed up for a quilting class with the amazing quilt
teacher and author, Harriet Hargrave. But knowing my
tendency to turn into a babbling idiot around famous
quilters, I sat myself quietly in the back of the room,
trying not to talk, drool, or do anything else embarrassing. After we began our projects, I felt Harriet near-
ing my table. "Be calm!" I shouted internally. "Don't
say anything dumb!"

Harriet spoke. "Your tension is a little high," she said.

I spoke back. "Why, what makes you say that? I'm perfectly calm," I said.

Harriet spoke again. "No, I meant your machine— your tension is set too high. You ought to lower it."

As I sat there, face bright red and ear tips burning, I hoped that I had suffered my final embarrassment. How naive I was then. Little did I know the humiliation that was yet to come.

Imagine this: I was invited to do a guest segment on "Simply Quilts" with one of my all-time quilting idols, Alex Anderson. I met her in the studio before the show, and she put me at ease immediately. She was warm, funny, and very nice. "No problem!" I thought to myself. "I'm going to get through this just fine."

Rehearsal went smoothly, and, all of a sudden, it was time to film my segment. The bright lights went on, and someone yelled, "Roll 'em." The familiar music played, and Alex stepped forward with the show introduction, which she performed flawlessly. Camera still rolling, she smiled and turned to me, introducing me to TV-land. It was now my turn to talk.

"Thank you for inviting me. It's so nice to be here, Alice!" OH MY GOSH! DID I JUST CALL HER ALICE?!? ON NATIONAL TV?!?

"CUT!" the director yelled. "Uh . . . Ms. Boyer . . . her name is Alex."

I could have left the studio that day actually walking upright if I had called her Alice only once. Trouble was, I was so nervous that my upper lip kept sticking to my teeth and I couldn't quite manage that "x" sound. I called her Alice one more time on film, then the director took me aside.

"Just try not to say her name," he said helpfully.

Sigh. I hope Harrison is free for lunch . . .

Grandma's Crummy Quilt Top

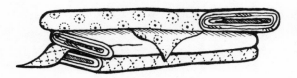

When my cousin recently acquired a long-forgotten quilt top made by my grandmother Jettie, she called me first. Grandma had died years before either of us was born, so we were quite excited to have uncovered this earthly link to our long-deceased grandmother. My cousin is not a quilter, but now she was inspired to learn. She asked for my help in finishing the quilt top and wondered if I had any ideas about adding a border. I was very happy to help and asked her to mail some pictures of the quilt top to me.

While waiting for the pictures to arrive, I did some research. My aunt remembered that my grandma Jettie was an avid quilter. She remembered that Grandma used to hold quilting bees out on her Arkansas back porch. The neighborhood ladies of Lincoln would come by, as would the women from her local church. The frame would be lowered from the porch ceiling, and the women would sit and quilt for hours.

I dreamed of my grandma and her quilts, wishing I could have been a part of her back-porch quilting group. I could almost hear the sound of the screen door slamming as each quilter, dressed in one of those amorphous floral sack dresses, would come through the door, accompanied by the aroma of her hot covered dish. There would be laughing and whispering, scissors clacking, and the occasional thread spool clattering to the floor and rolling across the wooden planks.

What a quilter Grandma must have been. She had quilted for decades. I closed my eyes and imagined her tiny stitches and attention to detail. My aunt was sure that Grandma had made hundreds of quilts, but few survived. As is often the case, her quilts were scattered throughout the community and our farflung family tree. This quilt top was a rare find, and we agreed that it was a precious family treasure. I had to wonder if my advice and skills would be worthy of Grandma's quilt top.

Well, you guessed it. The pictures that arrived in the mail were quite a surprise! Our precious family quilt top was constructed of plain muslin blocks and plaid nine-patches surrounded by small purple squares. At least I think they were squares—it was actually a little hard to tell. The quilt top was discernibly larger on one end than the other, the seams were wobbly, and the

entire quilt bulged like a circus tent in the middle.
There wasn't a single point that wasn't swallowed up
by an errant seam allowance.

Oh, how I loved my wonderful grandma at that
moment. Grandma wasn't an ol' fussypants! She was a
quilter just like me! She loved colors and quilting and
friends and porches. She didn't stress out herself or her
friends about their seams. At that moment, I felt a con-
nection with my grandma that defied the fact that we
had never laid eyes upon each other. My grandma
made dorky quilts, just like mine.

A few of my friends offered that maybe Grandma's
eyesight was bad. Perhaps this quilt top was one of her
first, or maybe she helped a child to sew this quilt.
Possibly it was a friendship quilt made by her unskilled
friends, they suggested.

All this might be true, but I prefer to think not. I
prefer to think that Grandma intentionally left her
descendants a message. I secretly hope that she was a
little silly, like me, and decided to leave behind a mystery. I imagine her wondering if anyone would ever
come across her funky quilt top and love it enough to
finish it. After all, she could have tossed it, given it
away, or somehow disowned it entirely. But she left it
behind, unfinished and imperfect, like some secret fabric time capsule.

Grandma, if you're listening, we love your wonky
quilt top. Whether the imperfections are intentional or

not, whether the message about imperfection is about you or about us, we'll never know. What a wonderful, mysterious, magical legacy you left for us.

As I write this, I am eyeing my box of UFOs and giggling about what horrible project I can leave behind to torture my granddaughters. I certainly hope they'll have a sense of humor . . . .

A Bad
Flattitude

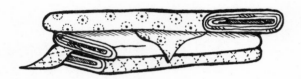

I know I've complained about depth and dimension before, but looking at the calendar, I see that it's time for my bi-annual rant. On this date exactly two years ago, I complained about this very same thing. And as nothing has been done about it yet, I think two years is a respectable amount of time to wait, don't you? After all, I don't want to add "whiner" to the list of descriptive adjectives on my resume. Too late? Good. No holding back then.

Why won't depth and dimension just leave me alone? Why are they always picking on me? I don't understand them at all. That's why I only sew flat stuff. I gave up sewing dresses in seventh grade. All those armholes and bust darts! Sewing lumps into nice, flat fabric just wasn't for me. After several disastrous attempts, I knew that making quilts was my destiny: nice, flat, low-loft, non-anxiety-provoking quilts.

The idea of "depth" in quilts especially puzzles me. When I look at something, I want to look *at* it—not *past* it—or even *through* it. It makes me seasick. Why do I need depth on my bed quilt? Why would I want to look past the surface of my bed? Or look "into" my wallhanging, for that matter? I know what's behind that wall: drywall, plumbing, and spiders. Ewww. Just give me some good ol' eye-stoppin' calico. I don't care to see beyond that.

What prompted my latest rant is that I had another run-in with my old foes, depth and dimension. I didn't go looking for trouble, believe me. I merely signed up for a quilt class. I was lulled into the class by the description of the class project, which made no mention of having to be able to function in the third dimension. The supply list simply required me to bring two color families of fabric, graded from light to dark. I grabbed some colorful florals and proceeded naively to class.

After spending a pleasant morning cutting and sewing our strips, we made some wonderful blocks. I was quite pleased with mine. I chose some acidy green prints and paired them with some lively purple florals. I imagined that my new blocks would make a nice lap quilt, maybe backed with some cozy flannel. Huh? What did the teacher say? Put our blocks up on the wall? What for?

The entire class, including Yours Truly, was instructed to put our blocks on the wall. Each student was to place her blocks on the wall, forming her own temporary "quilt." As the students stepped back from the wall, a lovely rainbow of colorful quilts surrounded us. But after a moment or two of inspection, we were astonished to see that the quilts actually had depth! Some of the blocks formed small, shallow boxes shading a central square. But some of the blocks had such amazing depth, that it looked like you could see all the way to Texas though them! (Unless of course you happened to live in Texas, then you could see all the way to . . . uh . . . Wyoming.) I was quite impressed. Here we were, making quilts with depth and dimension, and we didn't even know it. The ooohhs and ahhhs rose up as we realized that the class had held a secret agenda all along. We had discovered how to create depth when we weren't even trying!

Well, some of us. I supposed you've guessed by now who made the only flat quilt in the group. Without even trying, I had made a quilt that defied the laws of physics. Despite intensive color-shading techniques and eye-defying block construction, my blocks refused to enter the third dimension. They just hung there, looking like victims of a vicious steamroller attack. Needless to say, I couldn't see Texas. I couldn't even see spiders. My quilt was flat, flat, flat.

It proved to be a very revealing exercise. I've decided that if I can't even be tricked into making a quilt with depth, maybe I should just give up and do what I love best.

Ah, how I adore thee, flat florals and squashed stripes. Oh, how I appreciate thee, two-dimensional calicoes. I banish thee forever from my sewing room, Depth and Dimension. No more guilt about making "art" quilts that are supposed to "do" something. My quilts just want to lie there, flat on their backings, and relax.

Okay, I've marked that one down on my calendar. Next scheduled complaint will be in two years. (Heh, heh . . . you *wish* . . . .)

Diary of a Wedding Quilt

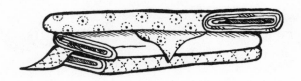

June, last year—I'm so thrilled! I've just learned that two of our good friends are planning to marry next year in June. Of course, I just *have* to make them a quilt. I know! I'll make it a scrap quilt; something that doesn't look like it came from a department store. I'm so glad I have a year to plan it.

November, last year—Well, I didn't get the head start I wanted to on the wedding quilt, but I'm ready to start planning now. I just have to finish this guild project, and then I'll be on to it.

January, this year—Gee, wasn't there something I was supposed to be working on this year? Hmmm . . . I can't remember . . . .

March, this year—Okay, now I better get myself in gear. I only have four months to make a king-sized wedding quilt. I think I'll do their quilt in warm, neutral colors. Fall colors seem to go with most people's decor. A half log-cabin design would be good, maybe with a braided border. I'll rotary-cut all the logs today. Let me see . . . that's only 1,064 pieces to cut. I should be able to start sewing by April.

April, this year—Whew! I got all my logs cut and I've already completed half of the blocks. I've run into a little problem though. I happened to speak to the bride's mother today and asked her the color of the couple's bedroom decor. She said, "Oh, that's an easy question. I just spent last weekend helping them paint everything purple." PURPLE? How could they choose purple when I'm making them an orange and brown quilt? Okay, not to panic. I'm only halfway through with the blocks; I can manage to throw a little purple in somewhere.

Later in April—This purple doesn't look so great. Adding some blue and lavender might help it blend in. And maybe some acid green. Yeah, that'll help.

May, this year—Hmmm . . . this is not looking so good. This purple is beginning to bother me. In addition, the blue and lavender look strangely lost, like they've accidentally wandered into the wrong quilt. But I've almost finished the quilt top and it's too late to start another. Maybe a border will help. Yes, a nice toned-down border will fix everything.

Mid-May, this year—What was I thinking with this border? It's too busy, and it makes the purple even worse! I shouldn't have made a scrap quilt anyway; I should have made a traditional quilt with muted soft tones of rose and . . . whatever goes with rose. No, I probably should've just bought them a toaster. Yes, a really nice toaster with no purple on it ANYWHERE.

Late May, this year—I decided to show the wedding quilt top to my sewing group. I felt so insecure about this project that I needed some kind words and encouragement. After I unfurled it, there was silence. "That's nice," they said noncommittally. "Is it too bright?" I asked, fearful of their answer. "It's a little bit bright, but it will be fine," they said. Uh-oh. Anyone who speaks "friend code" knows that "a little bit" means "a lot," and "it will be fine" means "I'm sure glad I don't have to give that thing to anyone I know." Now I'm really depressed.

Early June—I decided that quilting with black thread might help to tone down this quilt. Unfortunately, I didn't think about how the black thread would show every single quilting mistake on the white lining. To make matters worse, my machine does not like this polyester thread and keeps making a "finka-finka" noise. With every "finka," my machine tosses out a little black thread-blob onto the bottom of my quilt! The back of the quilt looks like a tiny hairy spider convention. Why, why, why didn't I buy them a toaster?

The day before the Wedding—A black binding completes the quilt. The black seems to be a very good choice, as it complements the black hairy quilt spiders oh so well. The black binding also seems to anger the purple even more, making it glow and pulsate with purpleness. The other fabrics join the angry purple mob, demanding: "How could you embarrass us like this? We looked so nice on the bolt! We had such high hopes for ourselves; now we have to spend an eternity with . . ." I really have to stop doing this to myself. Into the box the quilt goes. Where's that wrapping paper?

Wedding Day—It'll be okay, it'll be okay, it'll be okay . . . don't panic. Just put the box down casually on the gift table and walk away. No one else seems to hear the purple screaming from inside the box. Good . . . now . . . RUN!

A week later (after the honeymoon and after the gifts are opened)—The bride calls me at home, her voice breaking with tears of emotion. "Oh, Lisa, the quilt is so beautiful! I love the colors and fabrics! It's perfect with our house! We will cherish this as long as we live. Thank you so much. We will love it always."

Oh, my sweet friends, you are so welcome. I knew you'd love it . . . .

Ask Not for Whom the Vision Blurs (And Maketh Not Thine Eyeballs Roll, Either)

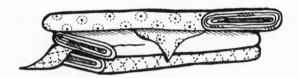

I suppose it's time to admit it. As I look around my sewing room, I see evidence of my insistent denial. I own 15 different needle-threaders and 17 packages of needles with big eyes, and my #12 betweens are sitting on my sewing table, unused and rusting. I guess it's time to break down and make an appointment with the optometrist.

You know, I didn't mind the wrinkles. I expected the wrinkles. I was content to call them "laugh lines" and slather them lovingly with cream every night. The tiny blue roadmaps appearing on my legs didn't bother me much either.

But I wasn't prepared for this.

Oh, how I remember being 30 or so, and watching some of my 40-ish friends juggle various pairs of glasses. Oh, how impatient I felt, waiting for them to find the right pair of glasses in order to see something. I avoided showing them printed matter because it would send them into a mad scramble across the room, searching for different pairs of glasses than the ones perched on their noses. "Oh, no, these aren't my reading glasses; these are my TV glasses. Here they . . . no, wait, these are for driving. Where are my . . . are these the ones? I can't see . . . "

"Oh puleeeeeze," I would think, rolling my good eyes. "Just go to the eye doctor and get ONE pair of decent glasses and wear them. How hard can that be?"

Heh-heh. I guess I shouldn't have rolled my eyes so much—maybe that's why my vision went blurry overnight. Or maybe it was that slow, controlled descent into my mid-40 that did me in. All I know is that on Tuesday, May 16th, I went to bed, confident in my ability to thread a needle. On Wednesday, May 17th, at eight in the morning, I arose to find that I could no longer thread a needle, glasses or no.

I phoned my older sister, who also happens to be an optometrist. "Help! I think I'm going blind! I could thread a needle yesterday, and I can't today! What's wrong with me?

"Hmmm . . . " she said. "You're old."

I did not like that diagnosis one bit. I would've liked a second opinion, but I didn't know where to get a better diagnosis for free. (Refusing to offer gratis diagnoses is a serious problem with doctors, in my opinion.)

So here I sit, weeks later, emerging from denial and descending into disbelief. I finally did go to the island optometrist. (Not free—but he didn't tell me I was old either. That alone was worth his fee.) My disbelief comes from my dawning realization that these glasses, which happen to be "graduated bifocals," don't work! Okay, well, maybe they work for reading and watching TV—but they don't work for threading needles.

Incensed at my doctor's apparent ineptitude, I had to go to the drugstore and buy a few pairs of glasses for threading needles. I bought a pair for threading #11 betweens, a pair for threading sharps, and a pair for threading my sewing machine needle. (I also bought a pair because they had adorable wild safari leopard spots all over them. Maybe they'll come in handy one day for hunting something—like misplaced glasses.)

Next, I noticed that these "graduated bifocals" make my stomach all woogly when I move around my kitchen trying to cook. How can I work when my peripheral vision is doing the hula? It makes me nauseous. So I keep my old pair of glasses, my "cooking glasses," by the stove, next to my emergency box of seasick pills. Then, of course, I have my "computer glasses," as well as my "double-strength magnifier half-glasses" for reading microscopic print on ingredient labels. At last count, I own nine pairs of glasses.

The worst part is that, despite owning nine pairs of glasses, I still find myself saying things like, "Wait! These aren't my sewing glasses; these are my jogging glasses!" and "Why do those inconsiderate 20-year-old-box-designers have to make this print so small?" as well as my oft-heard wail: "Can anyone living on this earth besides *OWLS* actually see these tiny VCR buttons?"

There is an amazing twist to this story, though. You may find this difficult to believe, but ever since my vision has gotten so bad, I've started looking years younger. When I look in the mirror now, I don't see nearly half the wrinkles that I used to. And the veins in my legs? Almost invisible now.

So as the years pass, I suppose I'll just have to keep acquiring glasses. One day, I'll probably have a different pair for every mathematical increment of distance known to womankind. Keeping track of all those glasses will be a challenge, but I'll just keep relying on this excellent memory that I've always had. Yep, my good memory will help me keep track of all those . . . huh? What's that you say?

Uh-oh.

My New Improved Seam Ripper

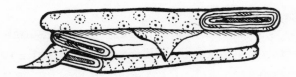

It's no secret that once a quilter becomes very famous, she can become a spokesperson for all sorts of quilting products. Some quilters win sewing-machine endorsements, some quilters have their own fabric lines, some even have their names associated with things like batting and rulers. As for me, if I ever became a famous quilter, I know exactly what product I would want my name to be linked with. I can already envision my elegantly scrolled name upon it, etched in gold: LISA BOYER'S ULTIMATE DREAM SEAM RIPPER.

I know what you're thinking, namely, "Did she say she wanted her name on a *seam ripper*?" And that's exactly my point. Why should we dislike seam rippers so much? My theory is that we associate seam rippers with our mistakes. They become a symbol of our human fallibility, a sign of our misjudgment and errant haste. Or maybe our dislike of rippers is merely because seam-ripping is so boring. Sewing fabric together is exciting; un-sewing fabric is just drudgery. We need to change our attitude toward seam rippers by making them more fun and exciting!

So it is for exactly this reason that I have been designing LISA BOYER'S ULTIMATE DREAM SEAM RIPPER. And in the best interests of quilters everywhere, I have decided to share my ideas with you. If any of you out there are involved with seam-ripper design and manufacture, please take note. You've been asleep at the drawing board for far too long, so pay attention to some Lisa Boyer ideas.

The first thing we have to change is the appearance of the lowly ripper. They all look the same. Some pretty colors would be very nice. You could have beautiful tortoise-shell covers, stripedy abstract blob designs, or you could even paint little dancing sewing machines on their handles. Better yet, give them an aggressive appearance. You could paint them up like tiny sharks or rottweilers with gruesome bared teeth. Give them names, like "Stitch Destroyer" and "Seam Meanie." After sewing a seam together incorrectly, wouldn't you just love to take "Rambo the Ripper" to it?

Seam rippers should be multi-functional. They should have multiple tools, sort of like pocketknives. Quilters have very little use for corkscrews and letter openers on their rippers, but we could use some other things. Like an M&M dispenser, for instance. Wouldn't

it be wonderful, if every time you had to use your ripper, a tiny piece of chocolate popped out of it? Or
maybe seam rippers could have little cell phones in
them. Every time you had to rip a seam, an auto-dialer
built into your ripper would phone a quilter friend on
your phone list. Then you could rip and commiserate
at the same time! "Oh Edna! You should see the star
points this seam just ate! I must have redone this seam
12 times already."

The best feature on my seam ripper would be the
tiny little built-in tape player. Many tapes would be
available to play on my dream ripper, but the most
popular tapes would probably be the motivational
speeches. The teeny-tiny tapes could play random messages on a loop, much like talking dolls, or your mother-in-law. They would say helpful things like: "Don't
worry, no one is perfect!" and "Every day, in every way,
your seams are getting better and better!" And my personal favorite, "My, don't you look slim in that outfit."

Or how about a ripper/CD player? You could play
music especially written for seam-ripping. I'm sure we
could get someone famous to record seam-ripping
songs like this one, sung to the tune of the "99
Bottles" song:

> Ninety-nine stitches to rip, don'tcha know?
> Ninety-nine stitches to rip!
> Take the thread out! No time to pout!
> Ninety-nine stitches to go! Ho! Ho! Ho!

I'm sure a country singer would jump at the chance to record these songs, as the seam-ripping theme lends itself well to wailing and moaning.

Oh, if I only owned my own factory. I would manufacture all sorts of useful sewing tools, most of them dispensing chocolate in some way. Hey! I just had an idea. What if the tool itself was actually made out of chocolate? That way, if the tool didn't work, you could just eat it instead. I gotta get down to the patent office!

If You Can't Say Anything Nice . . .

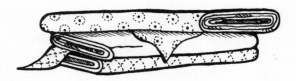

Ahh, a quiet, peaceful Saturday afternoon. My house-work is done for the week and I've earned some serious quiltmaking time. I locate my sewing glasses, pour myself an iced tea, and climb the stairs to my sewing room. Let's see, I think I'll listen to some classical music today, since I'm making some traditional blocks. What would go well with Lemoyne Stars? Chopin, I think.

An hour flies by, and my completed stars are assembling on my design wall. I have enough blocks to start playing with some layout ideas, so I juggle a few blocks and add some experimental sashing strips. Stepping back, I ponder my choices.

My husband walks into the room. He approaches quietly, as he can see that I'm deep in thought. Standing beside me, I can feel he's wanting to ask a "where's the . . ." question, but the new quilt top on the design wall temporarily captures his attention.

"That's a nice one," he says. "This part over here looks like . . . ."

"OUT! OUT!" I yell, before he can say another word. "Don't say anything! What are you looking for? I'll go help you find it! Are you hungry? Do you want something to eat? What can I do for you? Let's go downstairs . . . ."

Tugging and pulling, I escort him down the steps. I find the widget he was searching for and send him back into his garage. Whew. That was a close one.

If my behavior seems rude, I guess I need to explain. Let me tell you a sad story about one of my quilts; then it will all become painfully clear.

Once upon a time, I found a darling appliqué pattern in a quilt magazine. It was a delicate picture of two entwined roses tied with a blue ribbon. I hesitated a bit before I attempted it, because the larger rose had 20 or more separate petals. Some of the pieces were no bigger than my thumbnail. But it was such a sweet little pattern; I just had to try it.

Weeks later, I finished the appliqué. It was very pretty. I cut the block into an oval shape and appliquéd an oval border around it. I liked it so much that I hand-quilted it with feathered wreaths and lacy loops. I mounted the entire thing on a piece of oval foam-core board to finish it. I thought it was gorgeous. I found my husband in the garage and showed him my masterpiece.

"Oh . . . how nice . . . a toilet seat cover," he said.

ARRRRGGH! No! It wasn't a toilet seat cover! But now that he mentioned it, that's exactly what it looked like. The size and shape were exactly perfect. He was right. I had worked for two weeks on a toilet seat cover. I could never look at that little quilt in the same way, ever again. After trying unsuccessfully to get the toilet-seat-quilt picture out of my mind, I gave up and hung it in the bathroom.

You would think, after this experience, that I would've learned. But no! Once, after setting some delicate "Crown of Thorns" blocks alternately with some colorful "Scrap Basket" blocks, I proudly displayed it for him. "I was thinking of calling this one 'Snowflakes from my Scrap Basket,' or perhaps, 'Baskets of Lace,'" I said.

"Hmmmm," he offered, "it looks more like 'Aliens Invade My Fruit Bowl.'"

Needless to say, I can't see the lace, snowflakes, or scrap baskets in my quilt anymore. Now all I see are attacking alien space vessels, viciously shooting their horrible death rays into unsuspecting oranges and bananas. (Of course, it's my son's favorite quilt now. He didn't care about it when it was just snowflakes and baskets.)

So now you understand why I try to head off my husband's comments. To him, my quilts are like some giant psychological ink-blot test, just waiting for his bizarre interpretation. It might be okay if he just saw bunnies and ducks; you know, normal stuff. But last week, I purchased some fabric that had a tiny, regular, fleur-de-lis pattern all over it. While watching me unfold it in my sewing room, he did a double take. Noticing his attention was drawn to it, I asked, "You like this one?"

"It's okay," he replied, "but I never dreamed you'd buy fabric with houseflies on it."

Did I mention, "Arrrrggh?"

Scenes from an Elevator

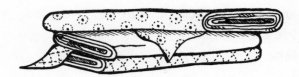

Years ago, during a visit to Sacramento, California, I committed a major faux pas. I actually *spoke* while riding in a crowded elevator with strangers. I think I said something like, "Gee, this is a nice elevator." To which the rest of the elevator crowd responded with a glaring sidelong glance and a nervous shuffling step away from me.

At that moment, a mischievous little voice inside my head urged me to start singing a Bavarian yodeling song at the top of my lungs, or perhaps break into a little elevator tap dance. I wish I had. But I didn't. I just clammed up like some loony old lady crawling with cooties, who accidentally had the nerve to speak while riding on an elevator.

I guess it was my fault. Living on the island of Kauai, I have very little occasion to ride on elevators, so my elevator etiquette was a little rusty. I also hadn't visited a big city for years, so I had forgotten all my city rules. "Don't talk to strangers" and "Don't yodel on elevators" were things I used to know, and I just forgot. I apologize to all those hapless victims who rode with me on that Sacramento elevator the day that I talked. You can relax; I'm home now.

This event was fresh in my mind last weekend, when I happened to step onto a crowded elevator. I was in a Waikiki high-rise at a national quilting event, and I could tell at once that I was on an elevator with quilters. They had the telltale quilted vests, the colorful sewing-related jewelry, the cheery dispositions, and the requisite bags stuffed with purchased fabric. They were smiling and happily chatting about classes and the marvelous quilts at the show.

I decided to do a scientific experiment. "Gee, this is a nice elevator," I said.

A chorus of enthusiastic replies broke out. "Oh yes, it is!" and "But they could use some different wallpaper in here," and even "Sort of a bumpy ride, though." The friendly chatter continued, and by the time we reached the lobby, I had been invited to lunch three times.

Oh, how I love quilters! Bless you all! I get misty when I recount this elevator story because it reminds me of how lucky we are to know each other. I have personally been graced with your collective warmth on many occasions, and now is the time to say thank you.

Stash Envy

In my married life, I have moved a total of six times, involving six different cities in three different states. Each of these moves required leaving friends behind and plopping down in a completely unknown environment. But as soon as the moving van was unpacked, I would call the local quilt guild. All I had to say was, "I'm new in this area; can you tell me where and when your guild meets?"

After the first phone call, I felt like I belonged in that city. Without exception, my call was answered by a guild member who was happy to hear from a new quilter in town. I was given directions (sometimes offered a ride!) and usually greeted at the door by a lovely mother hen who was appointed to introduce me to guild members.

How amazing it is to walk into a room and be greeted by hundreds of instant friends! There's nothing like it. A roomful of people who share so much: love of color and design, love of fabric, love of getting together and learning new things about our art. Even though I didn't know any of you individually on those first visits, I knew a lot about you, just by virtue of the fact that you were there. Thank you for taking me in. I'll never forget your kindness.

By the way, when does your elevator-yodeling minigroup meet? Can I bring my tap shoes? Can we go to Sacramento?

Fired from the Quilt Factory

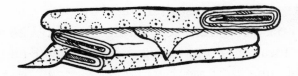

Have you ever dreamed of working in a factory?
From nine to five, your job would be screwing bottle
caps onto bottles or perhaps sorting buttons. Maybe
you could watch an endless parade of jellybeans roll by
on a conveyor belt and pick out the misshapen ones.
You might even get to pack widgets, pluck chickens, or
tie little ribbons on handkerchief boxes for eight hours
straight, day in and day out. Does this sound like the
kind of job you would like?

If it does, you're certainly not alone. Many people
like factory work, and I am grateful to them. They are
patient and steadfast and part of the backbone of
America. Without them, our quality of life would be
greatly diminished. Thank you, factory workers.

I wonder why I don't have that kind of patience. By
the time the fifth imperfect jellybean rolled by, I would
be in a daze. I'd probably have to invent little mind

games to keep myself from slipping into a coma. For example, on Wednesdays I could try to find the one misshapen jellybean that most resembles Elvis. I could alternate, finding early Elvis on even-numbered Wednesdays, and post-1970 Elvises on odd Wednesdays.

Nope. I can feel the stupor molecules lining up behind my eyeballs just thinking about it.

I feel the same way about string-piecing. Whoever got the idea that quiltmaking should emulate an assembly line? Not me. I get panicky when I read instructions like this:

1. Rotary-cut 56,000 light squares.

2. Rotary-cut 56,000 dark squares.

3. Sew squares together in chains.

4. Cut squares apart. Don't open blocks and look at them; it'll slow you down.

5. Place mountainous pile of squares on the left side of your sewing machine, with dark squares facing 32 degrees north-by-northwest relative to the south end of your sewing space. Pick up each square using your right hand, rotating it counter-clockwise as you go, simultaneously flipping it to the wrong side in a southwesterly motion.

6. Sew squares together again. No moaning. Or peeking. If you peek, your hair will turn into snakes.

7. Cut squares apart. Two quilt demerits for heavy sighing. (*I heard you!*)

8. Program the phone number to Happy Acres onto speed dial.

9. Oops! Did I say north in Step 5? That's only in the Southern Hemisphere. Got your seam ripper handy?

It's just too hard for people with brains like mine. (I've always believed that if someone cross-sectioned my brain, they would find a popcorn machine up there. "Pop! Hey . . . an idea! Pop! Pop! Another idea. Pop-pop-pop-pop! Uh-oh . . . trouble ahead . . . .")

Having a popcorn brain like mine presents some piecing challenges. For instance, I am a chronic peeker. Sometimes I can't even wait until the seam is finished. Yes, I'm a compulsive mid-seam peeker. And there is positively no way on earth that I can make 50 blocks at once. I usually make one block, stick it to my design wall, and then go eat a victory donut. If I'm inspired by the block (or the donut), I can manage three more. Now I have four whole blocks on my design wall— which I play with for a half-hour. Then I decide that I'm tired of the fabrics I've used. I add some different fabrics and go eat another congratulatory donut. My next 50 blocks are painful ordeals, done in at least 20 batches with 15 mind-changes. I won't even tally up the donuts.

I wonder why no one makes piecing instructions for short attention spans. Maybe it's finally time for all of us Popcorn Brains to unite. Like fed-up factory workers, we could demand shorter piecing chains and more peeking per project. We could stubbornly refuse to finish a quilt top with the same fabrics we started with. Or we could start a quilting revolution to do the unthinkable: make one block at a time. (Gasp!)

Or not. What was I talking about? Oh yes, short attention spans.

Perhaps I should just stop whining and learn to appreciate the genius of these mind-numbing time-saving techniques. I'm sure that eventually, I'll learn to live with acute sensory deprivation madness and its colorful hallucinations. Hey! Maybe this way, I'll finally get to talk to Elvis!

A Colorful Vocabulary

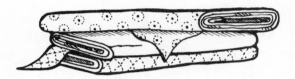

I've often heard that Eskimos have over 100 different words for snow. This is because, needless to say, snow is important in the life of an Eskimo. They have to build with it, walk on it, drive through it, and lots of other things that I can't even imagine because I live in Hawaii. I am only familiar with two types of snow: One type is the stuff that builds up in my freezer, letting me know it's time to defrost. The other type of snow I'm acquaint-ed with is the kind I see on television and in movies.

People standing in real snow on television always have that same look: slitty eyes, runny red noses, and goofy hats. They breathe out white fog and stomp about, flapping their arms and generally looking quite uncomfortable. This leads me to believe that, although they may not have 100 words for snow, they must have a snow vocabulary quite different than mine, some of which may be quite unprintable here.

Stash Envy

I often think of Eskimos and their snow words when I am trying to select fabrics for my quilts. We quilters need to follow the Eskimo example and come up with an expanded vocabulary of color. Oh, I'm not talking about impractical color words like "mango," "taupe," and "willow." These words are not specific enough, and men always tease us about them. To add to the confusion, some words pertaining to color are regional. I haven't seen a willow tree in years, so how do I know what sort of brown a "willow" is? I don't think I've ever seen a "taupe," unless it was one of those stripedy horned animals at the zoo. And do you really know what color "mango" is? I've seen real mango fruit in every shade of yellow, pink, red, orange, purple, and magenta. "Mango" can be any-thing, even brown or black, if you leave them in the refrigerator too long.

We need a system of color that is less descriptive and more practical. This is why I have invented my own system, which I will generously tell you about here. My system starts with the basic colors that most of us agree upon, i.e., red, yellow, green, etc. Then we blend the words, just as we blend the colors. For exam-ple, is your blue a blue-green? If so, it's a "bleen." Or is your blue more of a blue-purple shade? Then it's a "blurple." See how simple it is? No more going to the fabric shop to pick out a red and coming home with a "rue" when you really needed a "rorange."

My system ingeniously gives us more colors without having to learn more words for them. No more trying to figure out what "chartreuse" is. And my system can be very subtle, too. Is your brown more yellow than brown? Then it's a "yown." Or is your brown more brown than yellow? Then it's a "brellow." And what if it has some threads of grey-black running through it? It can be "brellow with grack stripes." No more dragging little scraggly snippets of fabric to the store for matching. You can just remember that you need a "riolet with globs of orey."

As a quilt teacher, I find my newly-engineered color vocabulary to be a real time-saver. When one of my students needs a fabric for a block, I don't have to stop and try ineffectively to describe the color that might work. I can simply say: "Go out into the shop and find a rink with a smudge of grue and a hint of peen." She'll know exactly what I am talking about. Well, if she comes back into class, that is. If I hear tires screeching out of the parking lot, I can see that she didn't quite appreciate the genius of my system.

My personal dream is that, one day, I'll be able to walk into my local quilt shop, and all the fabrics will be arranged and labeled according to my vision. All the plues will be separate from the blinks; all the whellows labeled differently than the wheys. Someday, I dream that I will be able to walk into a fabric shop and ask, "Where are your blurples?" and they won't laugh.

Stash Envy

They'll just point out a rack between the bleds and the grues.

I'm confident that eventually my system will catch on, much like the metric system in America. Eskimos will sit around their fires at night and tell stories of how many words we quilters have for different colors. And I will have done my part for quilting history once again.

Stash
Envy

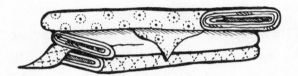

I'll never forget the first moment I found out I was
. . . uh . . . insufficient.

It was the evening that I held my first quilt mini-
group meeting at my house. I was new to the guild
experience, and I was delighted to be chosen as the
first host for a new mini-group meeting. I had tidied
my house, lit the candles, put out the guest towels,
and made a fabulous dessert. The day before, I had
spent the day cleaning and sorting my sewing room,
trying to tame the chaos a wee bit. Somehow, I knew
that my sewing room would be on the quilters' tour of
my house, so I had put some effort into pretending I
was well organized. I hoped I wouldn't crack under the
strain of maintaining the charade until much later in
the evening, perhaps after the chocolate dessert was
served. Yes, after the chocolate, they would like me no
matter what.

Stash Envy

As I fluffed the freshly cut flowers and added another log to the fire, the doorbell rang. My guests had arrived! One by one, they shook off the cold and settled into my living room where we had a very nice meeting. We told stories, shared projects, and generally enjoyed each other's company. Sure enough, one guest quilter asked, "So where's your sewing room? Can we have a tour?"

I led them up the stairs to my humble sewing room. Nothing fancy, just your basic 8' x 10' room with a sewing machine, sewing table, and ironing board. There was a polite pause, and then someone asked, "Where's your fabric stash?"

I pointed to a small shelf on the wall. "It's right there," I said proudly.

Silence fell. Fifteen pairs of eyes slowly met mine. Connie then spoke for the group: "Wh . . . where's the rest of it?" she asked in a trembling voice, her world visibly shaken.

Having been a lone quilter for most of my quilting life, I had no idea what she was talking about. Who would ever need more fabric than what one's current project required? Why, that would be wasteful! Did these women have more fabric than they needed? Why were they all looking at me with those huge, sympathetic eyes? What was I missing here?

"Who wants chocolate!?!" I sang out, breaking the terrible tension in the room. Thirty feet stampeded back down the stairs, forgetting the traumatic event.

Whew. Chocolate solves another crisis! (Is there anything it *can't* do?)

Needless to say, I became educated very rapidly when I began going to other members' houses for meetings. I remember vividly standing in my friend Jo's hallway, staring at the vast array of fabric along the wall. "Wow, Jo! Look at all your fabric!" To which Jo replied, "Oh, that's just the cat-fabric section. Keep on walking. Dots and stripes are in this room; solids in the next. Don't miss the batiks in the spare bath."

Now that I've been educated, I have acquired a bit more fabric. Unlike Jo though, I certainly do not have a wing of my house devoted to tone-on-tones. I think my husband's unreasonable insistence on having somewhere to sleep is cramping my style.

Speaking of my husband, he recently walked into my sewing room and surveyed my vast wall of fabric. "Gosh," he said, "you must have a hundred dollars' worth of fabric in here!"

If you don't tell him, I certainly won't.

The Two O'Clock Syndrome

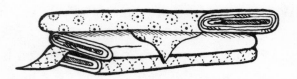

The first half hour of quilt class is utter pandemonium. Quilters are running everywhere. Some are making multiple trips to their car trunks, lugging in machines, mats, and rulers. Other quilters are busy scouting out electrical outlets, searching for last-minute fabrics, plugging in irons, and scrambling for seats closest to the coffee machine. Then comes the ceremonial arrangement of the mat, rotary cutter, paper scissors, fabric scissors, pincushion, and coffee cup. As I soundlessly pass out the class handouts, the students re-check the careful positioning of their sewing implements. Moments before I speak, the class falls into attentive silence.

A couple of hours later, the quilt students are on their individual quilting missions. Machines hum as students begin to sew. Thankfully, the heavy thinking phase is over and the chatting phase begins. New acquaintances are made; spontaneous laughter erupts intermittently. The over-achiever has finished all of her blocks and awaits my further instruction. The fabric-buyer is almost finished buying fabric . . . uh-oh . . . maybe not. She didn't see that pile of batiks over there. We'll see her after lunch.

Lunchtime! Everyone grabs sweater and purse and heads out the door in groups of two, three, and four. The over-achiever decides she's not hungry, and may she stay in?

At approximately one o'clock, the students wander back in from lunch, trying to regain the enthusiasm they had when their stomachs weren't quite so full. They wander over to their sewing machines and resume piecing, somewhat sleepily. Some re-locate their lost coffee mugs under piles of fabric. Irons begin making mysterious clicking noises while they re-heat. The pleasant hum of a swarm of sewing machines once again fills the air.

Uh-oh. Two o'clock is approaching. How I dread that hour. I watch the clock nervously, knowing with fearful certainty what will transpire. I anxiously scan the faces of my students for the first furrowed brow, the first machine to stop running, the first folded arms across the chest. Oh no, here it comes! The first student succumbs!

"Gee, I used to like these fabrics. Now I just don't know. This green is bugging me. I don't like my purple anymore, either. And this dorky floral—I'm about to skewer it with my seam ripper! Why are everyone else's blocks so great and mine are so *yucky*?"

And so it begins. The Two O'Clock Syndrome. The two o'clock question rises up like an ominous dark cloud from each quilter: Everyone else's blocks are so beautiful; why are mine so dull/boring/awkward/gruesome/ horrible? (Pick an adjective; I've heard them all.)

I wish some really smart brain scientist would do a study on this. Why does everyone dislike their own blocks at two o'clock? I suspect something finally shorts out in our eye-brain circuit, turning the colors we've been staring at since 9:00 a.m. to the spectrum of colors one would find in a bowl of week-old oatmeal.

The frightening part of this recurring scenario is the irrational decisions that take place after a quilter stares at her own moldy oatmeal. After all, quilters love color. The solution to her horrible blocks must be to just add more color. She thinks her blocks need some screaming orange and shrieking yellow. And maybe just a touch of iridescent Christmas plaid. Yes, that's it! Plaid solves everything at two o'clock.

Many quilters emit a distinctive "I hate my fabric" cry, and I can head them off early. But some students can suddenly leap up from their machines without warning and make a beeline for the door. To counter this infectious process, I station myself at the class-room exit. Leaving class with a purse is forbidden at this point. Clever students claim they need to go to the restroom, but if there's fabric along the way, I give them a lie-detector test. Most slink back to their seats.

The good news is that this syndrome usually clears up after 24 hours. The next day at home, the quilting student unpacks her class blocks and begins to appreciate them again. "My blocks aren't so bad after all," she says, while digging a hole in the backyard for the glowing bag of screaming plaids that kept her up all night. "Teacher Lisa was right after all."

Ah, how I love teaching . . . except at two o'clock.

My Inspiration

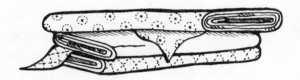

Although I love to attend lectures given by well-respected quilt artists, I must admit I'm getting a little discouraged. Oh, it's not their gorgeous quilts that intimidate me; it's their answers to common quilting questions that make me wonder if I should take up knitting instead. As artists, they think so differently than I do. I'm beginning to think that I don't belong in quilting at all.

I suppose it's my own insecurity as an "artist" that bothers me. When I first began quilting so many years ago, my dream was to make a nice, soft, fluffy, blanket. The "fluffy" part was the most important to me, so I went to a car upholstery shop and bought the fluffiest stuff my sewing machine could chew. I remember being so excited about my fluffy stuff that I almost forgot to buy the fabric to cover it. I dreaded having to go to a fabric store, having been held hostage in those places by my mother for many long hours during my childhood. But I finally dragged myself into one of those huge fabric warehouses (where old fabric goes to die) and picked out some remnants. Colors? Oh, who cares? Brown and . . . uh . . . more brown; that should do it.

Into my first quilting class I proudly marched, having to wrestle my giant fluff ball through the doorway. I was pretty full of myself, carefully eyeing the other student's puny batting rolls with sympathy. Fabric? Oh, yeah! I left that stuff in the car. Do I need it for this class?

So it was quite a shock to me, after a few years of making fluff covers, that I was now considered a "fiber artist." Whaaat? How did that happen? How did I, a nerdy scientist who couldn't even draw a diagram of a hydrogen atom, become something with the word "artist" in it?

After I started designing my own quilts (and using thinner batting!), I thought I would finally feel more like an "artist." Nope. I still didn't think like any artist I ever saw on TV. For instance, when I look at 3-D quilt embellishments, I still don't think of "textural interest"; I think of how much dust those fru-fru things are going to collect. I still don't think, "This yarn will add surface dimension." I think, "What's this stuff going to look like after it shreds off in the Maytag?"

Stash Envy

I suppose the critical issue that separates me from real fiber artists is the way I answer the question, "Where do you get your inspiration?" You see, real artists always seem to say, "nature." They draw their palettes from the autumn sky at equinox. They see form and texture in a forest stream. They look to flowers to inspire flowing lines.

My inspiration comes from somewhat different sources. To me, there's nothing more inspiring than a pile of dirty laundry. A pile of dirty laundry inspires me to go into my sewing room so I can forget all about it. A joyful flow of creativity follows, its duration depending on how much laundry there is. And if there's any ironing to follow, a personal artistic breakthrough is sure happen. Some artistic breakthroughs are so spontaneous and important that they actually require dinner to be prepared by the local pizza parlor. There is nothing more inspirational than the opportunity to avoid food preparation, I say.

Phone calls can be inspiring, too. My personal favorite is the "We're about to open the doors to the quilt show—and there's a big white wall where your quilt should be" phone call. There's also the "Margaret's baby shower is today—what did you get for her?" phone call.

I guess, looking back on it, I have evolved somewhat as an artist. I started out being inspired by 50-lb. polyester batting, after all. Now, at least, I'm inspired by laundry and threatening phone calls. (Not to mention those little voices that come out of the electrical sockets at night.) Is that progress? Maybe. But one day, I dream of being able to step outside and say, "I think I'll quilt what that sunset means to me," and be able to do it, even if I represent it with traditional blocks. Maybe then, I'll call myself an "artist."

Here, Spot!

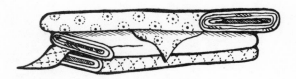

For all of you quilters out there who have special bonds with your favorite fabrics, you will not be shocked to learn that I have given a pet name to one of my fat quarters. But even the most seasoned fabric-lover among you may raise an eyebrow when I confess that I have actually *trained* my aforementioned fat quarter to perform a trick. To those of you on a cordial basis with your stash, allow me to introduce you to my talented and amazing fat quarter, "Spot."

I found Spot on a remnant table in 1987. I had only been quilting for a short while and hadn't yet developed any discernible taste in fabric. I favored the remnant table because I had a theory that if I was clever enough, I could make *any* fabric look good in a quilt. (Unfortunately, after several years of careful testing, I found that my theory was flawed. This was probably due to "clever" being the operative word in my hypothesis.)

Spot stood out on the remnant table. She had a color and pattern different than any of the other fabrics in the entire store. This fact alone should have set off the "QUILTER BEWARE!" warning bells in my brain, but my QWAS (Quilter's Warning Alarm System) wasn't fully operational at the time. I bought Spot anyway, all the time wondering what that distant clanging sound was.

As soon as I brought Spot home, I knew she was going to be trouble. As I tried to settle her into her new home on my fabric shelf, she refused to "Stay!" She didn't want to "Sit!" with any of my other greens, and my other pinks let out a shriek of protest when she came near them.

As hard as Spot was to place on my shelf, she was even harder to use in a quilt. I wish I could describe Spot to you, but, you see, that's part of the problem. I don't know exactly *what* Spot is. I suppose if you squinted your eyes, you could almost pretend that she's some sort of dotty floral. She's got green vines—no, wait, more like blue vines—with little pinkish-orange flowers. But open your eyes, and the flowers melt into little blobs of chewed gum on hot green asphalt. Perhaps she's a depiction of some sort of lush garden landscape—on a planet far, far away. Bluntly put, Spot is a real "dog" of a fabric.

Over the years, I tried to make Spot "Lay!" in a quilt, but she wouldn't have any of it. I gave up on Spot; I thought she was untrainable.

So when a fat-quarter exchange was announced at my local guild, I sensed a wonderful new opportunity for Spot. Maybe some other quilter, more patient than I, could find a nice, permanent, quilty home for my difficult pet. I tied a little ribbon around Spot's midsection, fluffed her up, and sent her off to the fat-quarter exchange. "Good-bye, Spot," I said, "and good luck!" In exchange for Spot, I chose another homely fabric, perhaps out of guilt for unleashing Spot on an unsuspecting fellow-quilter.

A month later, another fat-quarter exchange was announced. Luckily, I still had the homely fat quarter I had selected in exchange for Spot, so I was already prepared. (I guess other quilters have their problem pets, too.) When the big basket eventually came around to me, I couldn't believe my eyes! There was my little rascal Spot, sitting perkily up in the basket, still sporting her charming pink ribbon and looking so adorably fetching. I couldn't resist her—again. After all, it's not often that you can train a piece of fabric to come back to you.

Spot and I have performed our "trick" several times over the past 10 years. No matter what fabric-exchange basket I toss her into—she comes back at the next meeting, wagging her little pink bow, ready to come home with me. If she ever starts looking a little shabby, I give her a thread trim and a shiny new bow and send her out again. (Funny, she doesn't seem to age a bit— maybe dyes from other planets never fade.)

I figure that I'm doing my fellow-quilters a favor by sharing Spot. Spot victims will never yearn for a bigger piece of Spot (undesirable—and discontinued!), and Spot will always be pre-wrapped and ready to go to the next fat-quarter exchange. My friends will never have to cut into their "good" fabric when reliable, homely Spot is around.

Good ol' Spot. I'm glad my fellow quilters think you're a dog, too.

The Complex Mathematics of "Should"

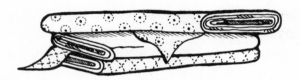

I have been avoiding my sewing room all week. I can't stand to go in because I have projects piled up in there that I "should" be doing. There's a stack of blocks that I "should" sew together in rows, even though I'm not crazy about the blocks. There's binding that I "should" sew on, and a quilt top that I "should" baste because the county fair is opening soon. And I really "should" cut the strips for my Christmas quilt sometime before Christmas Eve. Sigh.

There's nothing more energy-sapping than staring at a big pile of "shoulds." I don't quite understand why all these projects, begun with such enthusiasm, decided to turn on me like this. Take this one, for instance. Oh, how I loved the border fabric. Oh, how I loved the fabrics I picked out for the blocks. Oh, how terrible the completed blocks look with the border fabric! But I "should" finish it, so there it sits in the pile.

The Complex Mathematics of "Should"

Here's another one. All I need to do is cut some gray setting-triangles out of this marbled fabric. That shouldn't be too bad. Just two short hours of rotary-cutting teeny-tiny triangles out of this depressing fabric, and then I'll be able to sew all 31,627 of them on. Who wouldn't want to finish this? I think I'll go weed the garden.

Fortunately, I don't have to face this problem very often. My "shoulds" only pile up to unmanageable levels and conspire to keep me in the garden once a year. It happens with such amazing regularity that I used to believe it was a seasonal phenomenon. But after spending many long hours weeding in the hot sun and thinking about it, I have come to the conclusion that it's much more complicated than that.

I believe my "shoulds" pile up according to a precise mathematical formula, which I call my "GQ/BQ" ratio. Simply stated, for every "good" quilt I make, I generate a certain number of projects with which I am less than pleased. The "good" quilts are easy to finish, while the "bad" quilts tend to accumulate in the "should" pile. My personal GQ/BQ ratio is approximately two to one. For every two good quilts I finish, I tend to manufacture an unfinished one that just lies there and says, "Woof."

But wait! There's more math. (Gee, it's hot out here.) We haven't figured in the guilt factor, or the "GF." This part is algebra. The guilt factor is highly variable; it's different for every quilter. Personally, I have a very large guilt factor. I have been known to finish quilts just because I didn't want to disappoint the fabric. So I can subtract my personal GF factor from my BQ pile, before I divide it into my GQ.

Do you have your calculator handy? Because now we have to figure in quilts that are subtracted from your BQ pile because of birthdays, weddings, and baby showers. These aren't really "shoulds" anyway; they're more like "have-to's." "Have-to's" are exponential functions and therefore require advanced quilt calculus. The equation is now GQ/BQ minus GF multiplied by . . . uh . . . or divided by . . . no . . .

Oh, never mind. All I know is that once a year, my "should" pile becomes hopelessly large and sends me out into the garden, where I am forced to make highly suspicious excuses in the form of complex mathematical formulas. I guess I'll just do what I do every year, which is to bake something chocolate and invite my quilting friends over.

(Brrrrring!) Me: "Hi, Eileen! This is Lisa. Bring the group over. I have something choooooooocolaaaate!"

Quilting Friend: "Oh hi, Lisa. Chocolate? That sounds great; I . . . hey . . . have you been out weeding again?"

Although they'll never admit it, my quilting friends are mathematical geniuses. They excel at figuring out "should" piles. They say: "Ooooooh, this one is beautiful! You must finish this one, but not with this border fabric," or "Oh no, I wouldn't bother finishing this thing. Toss it and don't feel guilty—it's blocking your creative flow!" They even know when to be diplomatic: "This quilt top would make a good backing for something . . . uh . . . better."

With one visit, my quilting friends increase my GQ/BQ ratio, subtract my guilt factor, and multiply my confidence level. My "shoulds" convert to "want-to's," and life is good again.

Einstein should have been so lucky. He worked for years on that Unified Theory thing, but never did figure it out. Turns out, all he needed was some quilting friends. Oh . . . and maybe some chocolate.

Quilt in
a Decade?

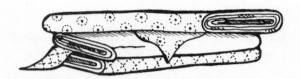

Earlier today, on this gorgeous fall afternoon, I plopped down in my overstuffed green chair with a cup of lemon balm tea and my reading glasses. I had been stockpiling quilting magazines for such a day: my house was clean, dinner was already in the slow cooker, and I was all set for some light, luxurious, quilt reading. Stretching out like a cat with a deep sigh and a contented smile, I felt myself relax as I picked up my first magazine. Ah, what future projects could I wistfully contemplate today?

After 20 minutes of perusing my magazines, I realized that my hands were cramped and my neck was stiff. I re-stretched, took a second look at my tea to make sure that it wasn't caffeinated, and continued reading. But I was having trouble focusing. I was turning pages, but I was no longer reading. I was turning pages faster and faster, and my feet were keeping time with an unseen drummer like they did when I took my last written driver's test.

I wondered what had made my relaxation disappear. Why did I feel so nervous? I looked down at the page I was reading and immediately understood my sudden anxiety. Here was a lovely picture of a simple pastel quilt with these words parading across it in bold print: "QUICK! QUICK! QUICK BABY QUILT TO MAKE!"

AAAAAAARGH! That was the problem! As I flipped back over the pages I had been reading, the same words kept leaping off the pages of the magazine at me: "FAST!" "JIFFY!" "SPEED PIECING!" and "Make this ENTIRE quilt in just TWO HOURS!!!!"

Whew! No wonder I was exhausted. And I felt guilty too, because according to this stack of magazines, in the 20 minutes I'd been wasting time reading, I could've made at least 32 quilts! What was I doing just sitting here? I should have been rapidly chain-sewing those 32 fast, speed-pieced, jiffy quilts! For all those QUICK BABIES! Who were so quick that they were probably in high school by now! Zipping teenage babies, pacing back and forth, tapping their feet, and demanding to know WHAT WAS TAKING ME SO LONG?!!!

I can get stressed out fairly easily. I've always been that way—the world moves waaaay too fast for me. This is the reason I chose quilting as a hobby in the first place, when I could have opted for oh, let's say . . .

stunt-car racing or high-rise bungee-jumping. (Not only do I not want to do anything really really fast, I don't care much for taking risks either. Having to eat my own cooking usually fulfills my risk-taking requirements for the day, thank you very much.)

What is the rush with quilting these days? Why are we in such a hurry? Is there an asteroid speeding toward earth that I haven't heard about? How did quilting become a painful activity such that we can't wait to get it over with—like sit-ups?

Count me out of the race. For me, quilting is a chance to meditate. All I have to do is sit down at my frame, slip on my battered silver thimble, pick up a needle, and . . . ah, I'm getting calm just imagining it. With my hands busy, my mind wanders off anywhere it wants to go. Hours fly by and I think about everything and nothing, completely at peace with the world.

I guess this is the reason that I choose the quilt projects that I do. I'm fascinated by complex piecing, odd shapes, lush quilting—all those quiltmaking techniques that make one wonder, "Oh my! Would I ever have the patience to do that?"

That's precisely what hooks me into a project: the patience required. I guess it's because I've learned that patience is something you don't "have"; you must create it yourself. It isn't a commodity doled out to all infants in varying amounts at birth. You learn (and earn) patience by making time for it, calming yourself down, relaxing, and letting it happen. The more you practice patience, the more you have. And the more you have, the easier it is to summon when you need it most.

Quilting is my anti-stress antidote. I don't want to go fast. I don't want to make zippy, quick, giant blocks in a speedy jiffy. I want to make agonizingly teeny-weeny blocks, one by one, savoring each color and piece, bit by bit. I want to do it leisurely, happily, blissfully, patiently. Let me sit here and quilt, enjoying those long stretches of time, rather than packing them so full they feel like an out-of-control bullet train.

Uh-oh. Speaking of out of control—my dinner's ready. Time to close the magazines, climb down from my meditation hideout, call my family to dinner, and serve them my special Creamy Garbanzo Bean and Brussels Sprout Casserole. Hey! Don't laugh! It's not so bad—if you eat it quickly in giant, zippy gulps while tapping your feet to keep your mind off the unusual flavor.

Maybe I should switch to reading cooking magazines.

The Making of a
Quilt Rebel

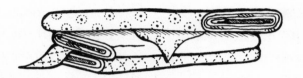

When I was first married, my mother-in-law gave me a very large and detailed book on etiquette. I politely thanked her and tucked the book away unopened, thinking that it might come in handy some day. After all, I would look pretty silly if the Queen of England happened over for tea and caught my shrimp forks out of place. So I put the book on my bookshelf and waited for the foreign ambassadors to call, or at least the White House.

After a few years, I came to the conclusion that the First Lady must be avoiding me. I believe that the CIA must have tipped her off about my cooking, which I think is very unfair. Taste, texture, and palatability are highly overrated when evaluating food quality. Why is there no appreciation for mystery? I make the most mystifying food around. It can look like chicken and taste like tofu. I am a magician when it comes to flavor. Poof. It's gone!

So since I wouldn't be hosting any state dinners, I decided that I would finally toss the etiquette book into the garage-sale pile. But before I tossed it, morbid curiosity made me want to open it to see what minor infractions I may have been committing all these years. What met my eyes was a shock. There were hundreds and hundreds of rules in there. They covered everything from birth to death with lots of napkin-folding in between. I was completely flabbergasted. How could someone write a book telling other people how they were supposed to do every little thing? Oh sure, I can understand rules like, "Don't chew with your mouth open," but "Never leave your cutlery on your plate in a crossed position"?

Opening this book finally put me over the edge. It reminded me of why I disliked rules in the first place. Anyone can write a rule. How can I be sure that the person making up the rule is any better than I am? I had never met the author of this etiquette book. What were her qualifications? Even worse, what if no one liked her? What if she never got invited anywhere because people were too nervous about inadvertently intersecting their spoons with their forks?

I gave the etiquette book away at my garage sale to an unsuspecting woman buyer. She tried to give me a quarter for it, but I wouldn't take it. Instead, I tried to remember her face permanently, as I planned to run the other way if she ever invited me to a party. Her expectations of me were probably already too high; she likely thought I had actually read that book!

Shortly after I jettisoned the etiquette book, I took my first quilting class. It is truly unfortunate for the quilting world that these two events coincided so closely in my life. Like an errant fork foolishly crossing a dessert spoon, my disdain for rules of convention crossed into my quilting life. Emily Post made me into a rebel; now the quilting world was going to have to deal with me. I wanted to question every rule, break every convention. I was on a mission.

In retrospect, I believe that if I would have learned to quilt during a later phase of my life, I might have gone along more quietly. In my later years, I have discovered that fighting convention . . . well, it certainly takes a lot of energy, doesn't it? So much easier to just go along, agree with everything, nod my head, and wait placidly in line. Then I go home, pick up my rotary cutter, and make a screaming lime quilt with wonky pink and orange triangles. Take that, Emily Post!

The Quilt Aftermath

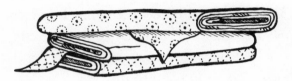

I stumble down the stairs like some mole-woman, the bright sunlight of day piercing my eyes like #12 betweens. As I wait for my eyes to become accustomed to the light, my sore, pricked fingers grope for the stair railing and detect a thick layer of dust. I make my way downstairs and pause to reflect upon a little pile of dead spiders in the corner. I silently wonder how many generations of spiders have lived and died since I last vacuumed. If the number of cobwebs is any indication, entire spider civilizations have risen and fallen, leaving their ancient history and architecture right here in my hallway. I feel strangely honored and repulsed at the same time.

I reach the family room and stand in the doorway a moment, gazing fondly at my family. My husband looks up at me from his paper. He says, "Oh hi, honey." Then he pauses a beat and, with narrowed eyes, asks. "Did you do something different with your hair?"

Hmmmm. Maybe I remembered to brush it today, but I think it's just longer than the last time he saw me. Or maybe he's referring to my upper lip, I'm not sure.

My son looks up from his video game. Pitifully, he gazes back at me with a squinchy face and trembling lower lip. "M-m-m-mother?" he asks. He's kidding, of course. Well, maybe. I barely recognize him either, as his clothes need ironing and he needs a haircut. I don't get excited that he's grown an inch taller—he does that every morning, so I'm used to it.

I dread the next segment of my downstairs odyssey. I can almost navigate my way to the kitchen by smell alone. There's a pineapple fermenting in the fruit bowl, and there are some tiny little flies that are quite happy about it. I wonder why husbands don't notice things like this. I don't ask him about it because I'll just get the Universal All-Purpose Male Shoulder Shrug with Optional Dumb Grin Attachment. (I recognize it because I do a pretty good female version of it when the car runs out of oil.)

I toss the pineapple in the garbage, much to the obvious dismay of the fruit flies, and approach the refrigerator. I grip the handle and brace myself. Nope, I can't do it. What if all those fuzzy brown vegetables had time to evolve into hairy creatures with claws and fangs? I just can't face refrigerator beasts right now; the spider tragedy is too fresh in my mind.

Plopping down on a dusty kitchen chair, I can't quite figure out how all this happened to me. It certainly looks like my house, only browner, webbier, and smellier. I suddenly imagine myself on black-and-white TV, with Rod Serling narrating my confusion: "One day, Lisa Boyer innocently decided to make a quilt for a local quilt show. Her deadline was a leisurely three weeks away. It seemed like a simple task, but at the end of those three weeks, she descended the stairs to find herself in . . . (pause for effect) THE TWILIGHT ZONE!" Ooky music would follow, along with a close-up of me looking bewildered and flabbergasted.

Truthfully, I shouldn't be bewildered and flabbergasted at all. This happens to me every time I have a quilt deadline. Then the last thing I remember is planning a quilt and reaching for my rotary cutter. And . . . WHAM! My houseplants wilt, my laundry grows to Himalayan proportions, and Rod Serling shows up in my kitchen.

I suppose a good solution to my problem would be to start earlier and to pace myself when I have a quilt deadline. That way, I could work on the quilt and still keep up with all of my housework—day in and day out, forever and ever, never-ceasing, never-ending, dull, boring, housework.

On the other hand, maybe the furry, brown, vegetable monsters are friendly.

A Practical Quilt Gift-Giving Guide

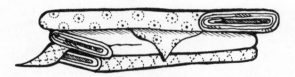

You've probably witnessed this scene: a frantic quilter rushes into a quilt shop, covered with threads and clutching parts and pieces of a quilt, desperate for a border or binding fabric. You can see the panic on her face as she checks her watch, mentally calculating how much time she has left. You note the impatient look on her face as the clerks seem to move in slow motion around her. Panic soon gives way to hopelessness, evidenced by her blank stare. Sighing, she resigns herself to sewing through the wee-morning hours. She also wonders if there is enough coffee and chocolate in the house to see her through the last stitch in the binding.

I can spot a quilter with a deadline a mile away. And to tell you the truth, just writing the above paragraph made me shudder and perspire heavily around my waistband. Quilt deadlines can be nerve-wracking, but I have learned to manage my quilt-related stress levels over the years with a few easy tricks that I will share here with you.

In my world, I have two kinds of quilt deadlines. The first kind is no problem: the quilt-show deadline. For some reason, quilt-show deadlines don't bother me very much. I love the whizzing sound they make when they fly past me, unheeded. Someone really ought to lecture me about this, but, so far, I have managed to look surprised every time I miss a deadline. (Please don't call the white-gloved ones on me, okay?)

The second kind of deadline is the real problem: the dreaded Quilt Gift Deadline. Oh sure, you may know about the wedding an entire year in advance, but just try making a quilt for the bride and groom. You will find that, instead of an entire year, you will only have 12 short months to finish the whole quilt! My best advice to you is to ask someone just as soon as you get the invitation to drive you to the wedding. You will need the time in the passenger seat to finish the binding. Also, buy one of those decorative gift bags now, because in your panic, you will forget entirely about wrapping paper. Take it from me; a lumpy plastic garbage bag does not look good on the reception table with all those silvery-wrapped wedding toasters. At least buy your bag a bow. And no, garbage bag twisty ties do not count as a bow.

Birthdays are not good quilt-gifting occasions. They come every year, so if you give a quilt one year, how are you going to top it the next year? You can't possibly give someone a quilt one year, and then give them a blender the next. They'll wonder what they did wrong. Do you want that on your conscience? No! Better to give them a nice, reassuring, friendship blender every year.

Never plan on making a quilt for a baby shower, either. Baby-quilt deadlines are notorious for bringing on early deliveries, sometimes after only nine short months of gestation. (Honestly, mothers can be so inconsiderate that way.) So instead of promising the mother a quilt for the baby-to-be, promise the new baby a high-school-graduation quilt. By that time, I'm sure that if you ask that 18-year-old baby graduate, chances are that he/she will want money instead of a baby quilt. How convenient is that, I ask you?

Christmas and Hanukah deadlines are the most difficult holidays to find late-quilt excuses for. "Oh, I didn't know Christmas was going to come again this year!" is not going to fool anyone. It will only raise suspicion and will lead him/her to question the integrity of your quilt-gift excuse. The best strategy for an unfinished Christmas-quilt gift is to turn the quilt top into a tree skirt. Practically anything can be a tree skirt, no matter what shape or size it is. Just wad the unfinished quilt top up around the bottom of their tree. Pile some presents over it and wear a huge smile. If you've only finished one block, buy them a miniature tree! A half-block could possibly be a tree ornament, but that's really stretching it. You've had a whole year, after all. And where's your quilt-show entry, anyway?

Doily Days

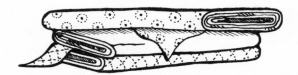

Do you ever have a bad quilting day? I do.

Of course, to put things into perspective, I should make clear that my worst day of quilting is still better than my best day of . . . oh, let's say . . . cooking. No, wait. I don't think I've ever had a best day of cooking. Let's say that my worst day of quilting is still better than my best day of laundry, which was pretty amazing: I had only one load that day. And it was all whites! Boy, what are the odds? Anyway, a bad quilting day is still far better than a good laundry day—even if you don't have to pre-soak—and I'm going to stand by that.

I often wonder if any of my quilting idols ever has a bad quilting day. Does Sharyn Craig ever have a day when she realizes that she has spent all day on a bad color choice? Does Judy Mathieson ever have a time when the gravitational constant under her sewing-room floor shifts, resulting in seams that will not align, no matter the physical force applied? Does Marsha McCloskey ever spend hours picking a seam apart, only to realize it was the wrong seam she just ripped?

Somehow I find it hard to imagine that Jinny Beyer gets herself into the same quilting predicaments that I do. When I sew a border on upside-down, I somehow imagine that I must be the only quilter on earth that is capable of such a dumb thing. Otherwise, quilters would be a far nuttier bunch. I know this from experience; that's how I got this way.

Fortunately, I have a strategy for coping with bad quilting days. Over the years, I have refined my strategy, which, I am proud to say, no longer includes the ceremonial flinging of the seam ripper across the room. I have, however, retained the traditional "stomping out of the sewing room," only because it happens to be a wonderful high-impact aerobic exercise, good for preserving bone mass in my hips. After 17 years of stomping, I have hips of steel. (No, what you actually see is their generous upholstery, not the steel part. Who asked you anyway?)

Now when I have a terrible quilting day, my coping strategy is this: I crochet doilies. No . . . really, I do. Remember doilies? Those white, round, holey things that looked like squashed snowflakes? Grandma used to starch them and set things on them, like flower vases and teapots. Our great-grandmas used to place them lovingly on backs of chairs and call them "antimacassars." "Antimacassars" must have been something Grandma used to prevent "macassars," which must've worked because I've never seen a macassar, have you? Our foremothers must have crocheted them into extinction. Whew! Thanks, Grandma.

Crocheting doilies is therapeutic. How can you stay mad at your errant quilt project whilst making a sweet, fluffy little snowflake? It's very healing. And if you make a mistake crocheting, you can just pull on the yarn and poof! Like magic, the mistake vanishes. No discarded fabrics piled in the trash, no tiny thread clippings all over your blouse, no needle-puncture wounds in your fingers, no digging your seam ripper out of the sewing room drywall. It's miraculous.

A wonderful thing about doilies is that they always come out looking just like the picture. You follow the doily directions, and your own doily comes out perfect, an exact copy! How often does that happen, I ask you? For me, nothing ever comes out like its picture. I've stopped buying cookbooks with illustrations; it's too discouraging. And my quilts never ever come out as good as the quilts in magazines, even though I follow the directions exactly. I'm starting to suspect that editors touch up those magazine quilts, just like they touch up supermodel thighs. They've got to be airbrushed! I have never seen a magazine cover with a lumpy supermodel or a lumpy quilt on it. Coincidence? I think not.

Unfortunately, quilters cannot live on doilies alone. After just a few doilies, I start longing for the excitement of colors and the sound of scissors. I suppose years of cottony fabric fumes have wended their way up my nose and into my brain. Once deep inside my psyche, the fabric molecules have become inextricably mixed with chocolate memories and other nice stuff I keep up there. My brain fabric atoms inevitably beckon: "Puuuuut down the doooooiilly! Come baaaack to your sewinggggg rooooom! You know you can't resist usssss!"

They're right, I can't. After a few hours of doily-therapy, I'm ready to face up to the cursed project that set me doily-making in the first place. At first, I cautiously engage in safe quilting. But hours later, I'm back to my old risky behaviors, like using plaids as backgrounds and sewing eight-way intersections.

Maybe I should crochet myself a nice straitjacket, since I evidently have several more years of quilting ahead of me. If I call it a poncho, do you think anyone would notice?

The Kind of Sewing Machine You Should Buy

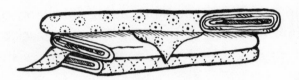

I am often asked what kind of sewing machine I use. As is the case with many simple questions, this one has a complex answer. If I could just say, "It depends," and move on to the next question, I would. But as a rule, students don't often let me get away with "It depends." I am sometimes forced into admitting that I own 15 sewing machines.

Please don't ask me why I have so many sewing machines, because I have no idea. I have a pink machine because it's so dang cute. I have a turquoise one for the same reason. I own a green one because it looked lonely in the thrift shop. There was an old black one I bought because it came with some great scissors. Then, of course, I just had to buy a light-weight machine for traveling, along with a spare in case of disaster. And then there are my loaner machines, sergers, long-arms, and garage-sale bargains. Amazingly enough, it all adds up to 15 sewing machines.

But instead of confessing to 15 machines, I have found a clever way to dodge the "What kind of sewing machine do you have?" question. You see, I have come to realize that the person asking the machine question is usually shopping for a new one for him-/herself. Besides asking *me* about a machine, he/she has consulted shop owners, consumer guides, guild members, friends, relatives, and the local gypsy. Why, I'll bet you're reading this article now because of its title. What you truly want to know is the answer to your question, "What kind of sewing machine should I buy?"

Of course, the answer to this question is "One of each." You should buy at least one of every kind of sewing machine available. If you have a favorite machine, buy two.

See how simple it is? But I suppose, like most people, you only want to buy one machine at a time. So your question is instead, "Which one should I buy first?" That's a little more complicated, and I'm frankly surprised that you're asking me. But since you've asked, let me give you a few tips that you may not hear from anyone else.

The first questions you should ask yourself are basic ones: "Do I want an oscillating or rotary hook? Do I want a 3, 5, or 7 mm throat plate? Do I need a twin needle delimiter feature, or is a manual override appropriate?" After you have asked yourself these basic questions, think: "Do I have any idea what I just said?" If not, don't buy a fancy machine; you'll scare yourself reading the manual. Instead, consider the machine with the colorful dots that read, "Thread Mr. Green next!" and "Careful of mean Mr. Needle!"

Never buy a sewing machine just to impress your friends. It doesn't work. Buy a refrigerator instead. My friend Penny has an actual refrigerator in her sewing room. She has snacks and cold drinks in it. It even has ice cubes! I was certainly impressed. She owns a Kenmore. No, not the sewing machine; the fridge is a Kenmore. I have no idea what kind of sewing machine she has. See? It works!

Don't try to shop for a new machine as you would shop for a new car. It's too easy to get overwhelmed by features you don't yet understand and mechanical things that you don't quite trust. Shopping for a machine should be a wonderful adventure, sort of like a date. Yes, that's it! Go shop for a machine and consider it a blind date. On your first date, ask yourself: Am I going to be able to look at this machine every day for the rest of my life? Am I going to be able to control it? How many owners has it had?

After you have dated enough machines, it's time to commit. Choose your machine as you would a spouse. Pick something comfortable and reliable, but fun. Make sure its tension level is appropriate. Be sure it isn't picky and doesn't complain when you give it a difficult job. Find one that likes to do a variety of things and loves to travel with you. See if it likes to hang wallpaper and if it will kill big hairy spiders. Oh . . . wait . . . .

Above all, realize that a sewing machine is just a tool! It won't make the quilts for you (and you'll have to smash the spiders with it yourself). Asking a talented quilter what kind of sewing machine she uses is like asking Rembrandt what kind of paintbrushes he used. The magic wasn't in his paintbrush. And I'm reasonably certain that the magic doesn't come standard on a new sewing machine either; although I really can't say for certain because I don't own *all* of them. Yet.

Zoning Out
to Quilt Land

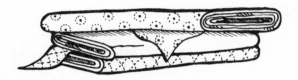

Yesterday, my husband began speaking with these words: "Metal fabrication is so interesting! Why, did you know that with the new zinc alloys . . . ."

Fortunately, I can't remember the rest of his speech. No, I didn't fall asleep or even walk away, looking desperately for something to dust. I remained seated, eyes fixed on his, even managing to look utterly fascinated by his recounting of the "History of Mercury Amalgamation in America."

How do I stand it? The answer is simple: when I'm forced into an extremely tedious situation, I think about quilting. Whether I'm facing a bank executive droning on about the virtues of a particular mutual fund, waiting in line at the DMV, or listening to my husband telling me about gear ratios—it doesn't matter. While my face is glued into the "I'm completely interested in what you're saying" pose, I'm really thinking about what border to add to my Ohio Star quilt.

This talent of mine required many decades of practice. I first noticed the problem of what to do with my brain while dating in high school. What are you supposed to do when boys start talking about car engines? How are your supposed to stay alert while they brag about the number of touchdowns they scored during the last basketball game? Not to mention all that talk about animals from different states, like the Los Angeles Goats or the Miami Porpoises or something. Not being big on zoology, I never understood why they cared about these animals so much. Perhaps they were endangered species or something; I don't know.

At first I solved my dilemma by changing the subject: "What do you think about hemlines this fall?" When I realized that they were as uninterested in hemlines as I was in carburetors, I thought the situation was hopeless. My next strategy, dozing off during dates, made me a very unpopular girl. I needed a new plan.

It was then that I decided to create the fun in my brain that I wasn't having on my date. "Oh, yes, Ted, please tell me about your spark-plug misadventure." Meanwhile, in my brain, preparations were being made. Lisa to brain: Prepare interested expression. Good. Nod head. Good. Okay . . . almost there . . . now. You're safe! You can think about eye shadow.

I wish now that I had discovered quilting earlier. We quilters are lucky to have something so entertaining to think about. Any time we are faced with boredom, we can just zone out and start thinking about the wonderful, exciting world of quilting. While a salesman drivels on about the virtues of his life-insurance policy, we can ponder our next quilting-tool purchase. During a dull movie, we dream about that new batik fabric we just bought. We can take a virtual visit to Quilt Land any time we wish!

Now that I have made the suggestion, I do need to issue a few warnings. First of all, never zone out to Quilt Land while you are doing something important, like driving a car or styling your hair. Don't run the risk of a car accident or a bad-hair day. Dreaming about new fabric while performing any task is hazardous. Save thinking about new fabric for those times when you are safely seated in front of an aluminum-siding salesman. Timeshare presentations are good for planning entire quilts, as you can easily outlast the salesmen. They will beg you to leave after nine hours—*and* you'll get to keep the free gift.

Second, please do your fellow quilters a favor and be discreet. Learn not to leap up in the middle of a family reunion while listening to Uncle Willard and shout, "Flying Geese! I'll do a Flying Geese border!" Keep your quilting thoughts to yourself. Otherwise, we quilters will never be invited to boring parties or tiresome sales presentations. Then when would be able to spend all that time thinking about our art?

So there is my . . . Hey! Pay attention! Are you really listening?

The Purple
Ribbon

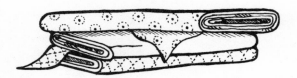

I, Lisa Boyer, was recently invited to teach at my first international quilt show. I wasn't one of the headliner "Featured Teacher" celebrity teachers, but by some amazing happenstance, I was asked to teach two classes. I was honored to be listed in the same brochure as some of the teachers on the class list, although I secretly wondered if the organizers had somehow confused me with some other Lisa Boyer. Maybe they meant to invite a different Lisa Boyer—perhaps a distant relative of mine—a confident, master quiltmaker, teacher-of-the-year type Lisa Boyer. Instead, they were getting me. Needless to say, I was having a confidence crisis.

All this was going through my head as I registered at the front table. The official smiled, asked my name, searched through the teacher pile, and brought out my stack of papers. Whew. They hadn't changed their minds. I was really going to teach.

After I signed my papers, the official handed me my name badge. Wow. My own name badge. I pinned it on, feeling very proud. She then checked my papers and pulled out a beige ribbon to attach to my badge that said, "Exhibitionist." Or maybe it said "Exhibitor." I don't know, because I was temporarily blinded by the next object she pulled out.

There on the table between us, she laid out a giant purple ribbon. It was glowing, and it had neon lights blinking all around it as it waved about on its own and played "Hail to the Chief." And on that amazing purple ribbon, emblazoned in gold, flashing Roman script and surrounded by flying cherubs with trumpets, there was one glorious word: TEACHER.

Well, that's how I remember it anyway. It may not have had actual cherubs hovering around it, but it was pretty impressive. So impressive that I was a little unnerved by the thought of actually wearing it. If you walk around with the word "TEACHER" on you, don't people expect you to actually know things? Now I don't know about you, but the prospect of actually having to know things really bothers me.

As she pinned my "TEACHER" ribbon on, I tried to think of some answers to questions. Which ones? I didn't know—I was panicking. As I walked away from the registration table, a crowd of quilters approached. Oh no! Quickly, I turned away. Did they see my purple teacher ribbon? I ducked into the nearest elevator, shielding my badge. It was a narrow escape, because I could sense that they had a complicated quilt math question for me. As the elevator doors closed, I heard one of them ask the registration lady where the dessert reception was. Rats! I actually *knew* the answer to that one!

Safely inside the elevator, I pondered my options. I could put my sweater on over it. No, this was Honolulu in July; I didn't have a sweater. I could take the ribbon off and stuff it in my purse. No, my purse was already full of fabric. Oh, how was I ever going to walk around with this thing on? How was I ever going to live up to its expectations?

While my mind was busily chewing on my cowardly options, my eyes fell upon the woman standing next to me in the elevator. She too, had on a purple ribbon, and she looked vaguely familiar. All of a sudden, it dawned on me. "You're Sharyn Craig!" I yelled. "Wow! I love your quilts! I have all of your books! I'm taking one of your classes tomorrow!"

"Wow!" said Sharyn Craig, one of my quilting heroes. "You're Lisa Boyer! I read your column all the time! I saw your "Northwinds" quilt at the show—it's wonderful! I can't believe I met you on the elevator!"

After the elevator stopped, Sharyn Craig and I parted ways, smiling and promising to have lunch. As I sauntered away from the encounter, I noticed that my purple teacher ribbon had stopped glowing and playing music. It had shrunk down from its previous gigantic monumental size to a more manageable one. As a matter of fact, it looked at home, pinned right here on me, Lisa Boyer.

Thanks, Sharyn.

As Long As It Takes

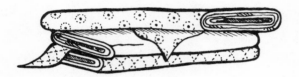

I've been quilting for almost 17 years. You would think that in all that time I would have figured out how to answer the following question: "How long does it take you to make a quilt?" But honestly, as often as I've heard that question, it still causes me to freeze up like the proverbial deer in headlights.

I know that, to the asker, it seems innocent enough. It's one of those smalltalk questions, sort of an ice-breaker question designed to start a real conversation. A person asks how long it takes me to make a quilt, and I respond with a certain time frame. I gather this information, of course, from the time-clock punch card that has been so conveniently built into my sewing machine. "Let me see . . . I'll check my time sheet for April . . . ah, yes, here it is . . . the blue Nine Patch . . . that would be 17 hours and 33 minutes."

Unfortunately, you can see what this question has done to me over the years. It has turned me into a hopeless smart aleck. Believe me, I used to try and answer this question in earnest. I would explain the differences between pattern intricacies, time taken to hand-quilt versus machine-quilt, time spent on creative planning and fabric choice, etc. But after years of watching eyes glaze over during my long-winded explanation, I realized that what the question-asker wanted was a short, snappy answer. So now I make up my answers. How long did it take me to make my king-sized hand-quilted Baltimore Album quilt? Twenty minutes. The yarn-tacked Rail Fence comforter? Thirty-two years.

I don't really mean to be a smart aleck. It's just that a funny answer is so much more interesting than the real answer. Even my former long-winded version of the answer with all its technical considerations wasn't the entire truth. Yes, a 64-point Mariner's Compass block does usually take longer than a three-stripe Rail Fence block—but it depends on a lot of other things, doesn't it? For instance: What day of the week did you start the Rail Fence block? If you start the block on a Sunday evening, and Monday is laundry day, the block is going to have to wait until Tuesday. And if you start the Rail Fence block on the day you promised your family something besides weenie roll-ups for dinner, just forget the quilt patch until the next day. And then there's soccer practice, potlucks, out-of-town guests, Christmas shopping, baking, canning, spring cleaning, and dental check-ups. How long does it take to make a quilt? Absolutely forever.

Personally, I am plagued by pesky alien invasions that take up a lot of my time. I'll put aside a quilt I'm stuck on for a few days . . . and then you know what happens, don't you? The quilt falls victim to the UFO aliens. The aliens drag my unfinished quilt to the Roswell Area in the darkest corner of my sewing room. Years later, after the aliens finish probing and testing my quilt top, they return it to me. I barely recognize it, because they usually return it looking terribly thready, haggard, and disoriented, but I finally sew on the border it deserves. Then I stare at it for awhile and decide to quilt it . . . in a day or so. Uh-oh. Here come those aliens again, their curiosity obviously piqued by the colorful new border. Add another two years time onto that quilt.

How long does it take me to make a quilt if there is no cooking or aliens involved? Hmmmm . . . how accurate an answer do my questioners expect? Should I include hours spent looking for my misplaced rotary cutter? Time spent consuming quilt-related chocolate? Minutes spent channel-surfing while I sew? Time wasted looking for a Band-aid? Hours of picking threads off my blouse and carpeting? See what I mean? That question is just too hard!

In truth, I secretly suspect that no one really cares how long it takes me to make a quilt. I think, especially after hearing the space-alien version of my answer, they're just amazed that I can finish one at all.

Quilt
Radio

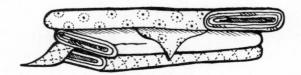

I lost my car stereo in a cupholder accident last year when I had to come to a sudden stop. I remember now that I was listening to "Girl from Ipanema" when a stop sign suddenly appeared out of nowhere. As I braked, I watched in horror as my ice water went on a beautiful arcing splash from my tippy cup directly into my cassette-player cavity. My radio shorted out, leaving me to wonder if that girl from Ipanema ever got where she was walking to—while all those people were saying, "Aaaaaah."

Having no stereo in my car presented a serious challenge for me and probably a hazard for you, since now you have to read about it. My mind wandered. I started wondering what a radio program for quilters would be like. It would certainly be interesting, because you wouldn't be able to see the quilt. You would just have to use your imagination.

I would, of course, be the starring radio host since it was my idea. I would invite women from quilt guilds everywhere to be my guests. I would be sure to invite nice, warm, wonderful, funny quilters whose quilts are . . . hmmm . . . how shall I say this? Artistically challenged? I think those of us who make dorky-looking quilts ought to have equal time and attention.

I wouldn't want to ask the same old quilting questions of my guests, either. No more, "How long have you been quilting and what kind of batting do you use" questions. Instead, I would be a hard-hitting investigative quilt journalist, asking the difficult questions we all want to know. For instance:

Me: "Gee, Margaret, your quilt, 'Ducks Flying Outside my Window,' is wonderful. Please tell our listeners how you came up with that original title."

Guest: "Lisa, that's actually a very interesting story. One day I looked out my window and saw ducks flying outside it, so I decided . . . ."

Me: "Margaret, that's totally fascinating. Tell me, have you ever been arrested?"

Okay, maybe that's a little too hard-hitting for my first show. Maybe we could start with the raging and controversial "steam or no steam" ironing debate. Then we could ease into some heavier issues, like: "Basting thread—what is it *really* made of?"

I would occasionally have well-known quilters, too, because I would have to prop up my credibility somehow. I would love to interview someone famous, but I wouldn't want to ask him or her the same questions she/he has to answer all the time. No more "Where do you get your inspiration from" questions, to which everyone always answers, "From nature."

The kind of questions I would ask would be more relevant. For instance, wouldn't you just love to know what Caryl Bryer Fallart brings to a potluck? Who was Sharyn Craig's first date? What does Jinny Beyer like on her pizza? Who would Sara Nephew choose if she had to marry one of the Monkees? Why does no one ask these questions?

After my radio quilt talk show becomes popular, I could branch out into television. I was thinking about a 24-hour cable show entitled, "The Fabric Channel." Quilters everywhere would be able to know instantly whenever a new fabric was rolled out of the fabric factory paint vat (or however they do it). Or how about a Christmas Seam-Ripping TV Special? You could save up your seam-ripping from all year long, then rip the seams while someone is singing cheerful Christmas tunes to you. Who could be grumpy about ripping while someone is singing the Frosty song?

You know, it's very difficult being a visionary without a car stereo. I wonder how Copernicus managed it. I'm sure *his* friends wouldn't take up a car-stereo collection fund, just because he mentioned a plan for a blockbuster suspense movie about thread tension. Honestly, I am *so* under-appreciated . . . .

Lisa's Machine Quilting Tips

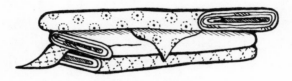

I adore machine-piecing. With the pairing of a rotary cutter and a quarter-inch machine presser foot, I must admit that I am often surprised and delighted by the accuracy of my results. How lucky I feel to be piecing in this era, with so many rulers, tools, and gadgets to help me attain such precision. My triangles keep their points most of the time, and my squares are getting more square-like every year.

Unfortunately, I cannot muster the same enthusiasm for the actual quilting of the quilt top. Unlike machine-piecing, machine-quilting is so inexact! It never comes out as I envision it. After many years of frustration, I have given up on machine-quilted artistry. Frankly, I do it just to get it over with. So knowing how I feel about machine-quilting, many of my friends marvel at the fact that I get so much of it done. "If you dislike it so much, how is it that you finish so many quilts and so quickly?" my students ask. So by popular demand (and with apologies to all the really fine machine-quilting artists of the world), I offer my six secret and valuable machine-quilting tips.

1. First, I select a machine-quilting pattern that I really love. I own a huge variety of quilting patterns, so this can take me a while. I try to choose a pattern that perfectly complements the design of my quilt top, yet is able to add its own quirky brand of charm to my quilt. After I select the perfect design, I carefully transfer the full-size design to a paper pattern, using a Number Two pencil. I then hang this pattern on my design wall and admire it. I ask myself: Isn't it lovely? Wouldn't it just be perfect? Then I crumple it up and throw it away. Mine will never look like that.

2. Next, I select an alternate design. This time I pick a pattern that may not perfectly complement my quilt top, but one that I may have a snowball's chance of actually achieving. It doesn't matter much what the design looks like, because everything I attempt pretty much turns out looking the same anyway.

3. After I have selected the alternate design, I re-name it. This is important because I have found that pattern names tend to set up false expectations. For instance, if I decide to quilt a motif called "Garlands of Daisies," you might expect to see a discernible

daisy in there somewhere. Why set myself up for disappointment? I rename the pattern something like, "Globs of Martian Flora," and I get exactly what I aim for. I am proud of the designs in my personal repertoire, which include: "Unidentified Swimming Things," "Overcooked Noodles in Space," and "Flight Paths of Drunken Bumblebees."

4. I like to experiment with a variety of threads. They all tangle in such interesting and original ways. Remember, thread can add an artistic element to a quilt top, especially if you leave in all the knots, loops, skips, shreds, and gnarly balls. It's called "texture"—I read that somewhere.

5. Before I sit down to quilt, I take a good long look at myself in the mirror and note two important things. The first is the approximate location of my shoulders. This information will be useful later on when I attempt to pry them down from up above my ears. It is a scientific fact that shoulders attempt to migrate upwards during the quilting process. Where they think they are going is a mystery. Perhaps they just can't take the stress any more.

6. The other thing I note *before* I sit down to quilt is that I have a smile on my face. I try to keep the smile in place during machine-quilting, even as my shoulders are making their mad dash toward the ceiling. Silly shoulders! Funny texture! Goofy thread

snarls! Drunken blobs of floral swimming things! How you make me laugh!

From here, I sort of zone out and the quilt just happens. I'm sorry I can't furnish you with more details, but I think I experience some sort of out-of-body experience during the quilting process. Or maybe it's some sort of schizoid break with painful reality; I'm not sure. But hours later, my quilt top is finished, my shoulders return home, and my sanity is somewhat restored.

Whew! Survived another one. Now I can get back to piecing.

"I Think
It Was Blue"

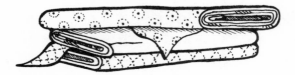

I adore quilting, and I have for the last nearly 17
years. Most of my friends are quilters. We love to get
together to make quilts, or just to talk about quilting.
I read quilting books in my spare time. And when I'm
not quilting, reading about quilting, or talking about
quilting, I teach quilting.

Yes, I am obsessed. But I don't often realize it until
I have an occasion to interact with non-quilting
humans. Believe it or not, there are still beings among
us who do not quilt. Oh, they look normal enough,
but their curious lack of dialogue when the discussion
turns to fabric will expose them every time. If you
should find yourself in a conversation with these non-
quilt-terrestrials, try to remain calm. Think of a funny
story about your bobbin tension and start to tell it.
That should drive them away. Then, as soon as possi-
ble, proceed directly to your nearest quilt guild for

debriefing. A stop at the fabric store along the way will soothe your shattered nerves.

I recently had one of these "other non-quilting world" encounters at my local bookstore. It was quite eerie. I don't mean to cause alarm; I didn't get abducted or probed, but I want to share my experience with you should you find yourself in a similar close encounter. Consider it a message from beyond.

This rather spooky tale happened when I was showing my quilts at a well-known bookstore. I made myself available for questions, assuming that I would get the sort of questions I was used to, like "What is the polyester/cotton ratio of this batting?" or "Is this a double-French-fold binding?" But I did not get the sort of questions that I have come to expect from quilters. Instead, I got peculiar and mysterious non-quilter questions like, "How long did it take you to make all these blankets?" or "Do you do altering, too? I have some pants I need hemmed." Arrrrgh!

But never mind the weird questions. The thing that really frightened me was one particularly freakish dialogue that haunts me over and over again. It happened during a conversation that started out pleasantly enough but turned nightmarish:

Non-Quilter: "Oh quilts! I love quilts. My grandmother made quilts."

Me: "Oh, that's nice. Do you still have any of the quilts your grandmother made?"

Non-Quilter: "Yes, I do. I'm proud to say that her quilt has been on my bed for 30 years."

Me: "Wonderful! What block pattern is it?"

NQ: "Pattern?"

Me: "Yes, a pattern—on the quilt. Are there stars? Squares? Rectangles? What shapes are on it?"

NQ: "Hmmmmm . . . shapes? (Thinks hard . . . pauses . . . scratches forehead . . . then answers) "Blue. I think it's blue. Or maybe yellow. I can't remember."

EEEEEEEK! Isn't that the spookiest story you've ever heard? He can't remember the quilt-block pattern, but he *"thinks it's blue."* Poor Granny! I imagine that the quilt in question is probably a hand-pieced, 128-point Mariner's Compass quilt with microscopic hand-quilting, spaced 16 stitches to the inch. It probably belongs in the Smithsonian instead of on his bed. As a matter of fact, I'll bet he lets his rottweiler sleep on it. Yes, that's it! He has a whole family of rottweilers who chew on Granny's quilt while he's away at the bookstore talking to strangers. How could he?

Okay, I know I have an overactive quilt imagination. Granny's quilt is probably a Dacron polyester yarn-tied comforter stuffed with newspaper. And he loves and values it enough to sleep under it every night and think about his beloved Granny. So now I really sort of like the guy, even though he can't even remember what pattern or color his quilt is.

So I guess the lesson I learned here is to keep my perspective. I can appreciate the art of quilts and teach how to make perfect points in my classes. I can get so immersed in the finer points of quilting that it takes a non-quilting alien with an imaginary family of rottweilers to teach me about quilting. It isn't the shape of the designs or the points or the batting, it's the love you sew into your quilt that is your true legacy. Go figure.

I Married a Nerd

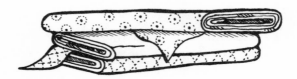

My husband made me into a potato clock today. Don't worry; I think it's only temporary, but I wish I were sure. I'm sitting here typety-type-typing away with a penny taped to my neck. The penny, in turn, is wired to a piece of a cat-food can, which is also taped to my neck. My husband explained that, whatever this thing is supposed to be doing to my neck, it works on the same principle as the potato clock. I forget what it is supposed to be doing; I don't want to ask because I didn't quite understand the two-hour version when he explained it to me the first time. I plan to get suspicious if he wires me up to anything explosive, but for now, I just take it in stride. I've come to expect things like this. I married a nerd.

I suppose I was always attracted to the geeky type. As far back as I can remember, those individuals who were a little "different" have fascinated me. There was

Darrell Parris in kindergarten, a kid who had very big teeth and a perpetually runny nose. Darrell was a 60-year-old man in a five-year-old's body. While all the rest of us were proudly comparing our brightly painted Spiderman or Barbie lunchboxes, Darrell solemnly carted his liverwurst sandwich to school in a double-decker, corrugated, gray box. He wore a moss-green cardigan sweater with wooden buttons and even carried his own handkerchief in his pocket. Darrell, whatever happened to you? I'm sure you're the head of neurology at some brain-surgery facility now. Or you're sequestered away in some think tank at Princeton, quietly solving Fermat's last theorem.

Sometimes I wish my geeky husband would spend more time in *his* think tank instead of visiting me in my sewing room. I enjoy his company while he's talking with me, but when he starts intently watching me perform some task, and then becomes strangely interested, that's when I start worrying. All it takes is one look at him to see the wheels turning in his head. He'll ask me a few innocent questions about the task I'm performing, and then, suddenly, he'll leap up and disappear. Strange and horrible noises will emanate from the garage. A few hours later, he'll reappear at my sewing-room door with a goofy grin, covered with sawdust, and triumphantly holding a *thing*.

My husband's creations usually involve wood, coat hangers, paper clips, and metal screws. Sometimes they include bits of ceramic tile, rubber bands, foam stoppers, and soldered coins. So far he has made me a thread rack, ribbon holder, glue stand, ironing board, and a gizmo that pokes ribbon pieces through plastic bags. Not to mention wrist-supporters, chair stops, fabric-sorters, collapsible table legs, and iron-cord holders. You name it; I have a coat-hanger version of it.

Ah, but if he would only stick to wood and coat hangers, we wouldn't have a problem. I start to worry if something he invents involves electricity. It's pretty disconcerting to be examining something he has made, and then, before he plugs it in, to have him loudly advise: "Uh, you might want to step back a bit." From previous experience, I move to the other room. If no explosions issue forth, I come back and take a look.

My husband's most recent geeky adventure involved an antique, industrial, long-arm sewing machine he bought at a yard sale. He took this 70-pound sewing machine, built it some wheels (uh-oh), mounted it upon a wooden structure resembling a picnic bench (huh?), attached some sprinkler pipes (oh, no), and wired the whole thing up to a huge belt-driven motor (gasp!). When I saw that this whole conglomeration had an electrical cord leading out of it, I quietly programmed 9-1-1 into the automatic dialing feature of our telephone and waited outside. Fortunately, the sparks that ensued were only minimal. And to my surprise, the machine-on-a-thing works great!

Thanks to my husband, I now have a marvelous quilting machine. To date, I have quilted over 20 quilts on it, with only minor injuries and a few singed arm hairs. My quilting may not be show quality yet, but I'm sure my husband will think of something.

I often wonder if Darrell married. I wonder what his wife must be like. I wonder if she's a quilter like me, or just another potato clock. In any event, I hope her life is as fun as mine—if she's survived it, that is.

My "Expert" Opinion

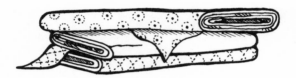

After my first book, *That Dorky Homemade Look,* was published, my husband turned to me and asked, "So how does it feel to be an expert at Dorky Homemade Quiltmaking?"

Huh? Me . . . an *expert?*

At that moment in my mind, I pictured a famous TV host turning to me and asking, "So, Lisa, how do you make a Dorky Homemade Quilt?" And I would say: "Well, Oprah, it's not really a technique; it's more of an attitude. You have to throw away your seam ripper. You have to learn to ignore your color wheel. You have to doggedly follow your inner voice, knowing all the while that it has bad, really bad, taste."

Somehow I didn't expect my life to take this turn. How did I end up an expert at doofus-style quiltmaking? I don't recall taking an aptitude test at Career Day for this.

Until this time in my life, I hadn't done anything remotely expert-ish. Until recently, my biggest talent was being able to pick out the perfect size plastic container for the amount of leftovers in the pan. I'm really quite good at it, if I do say so myself. My friends test me on it, and I amaze them every time. (My sister has an amazing talent also. She is able to look at a shoe, any shoe, and predict its exact size with uncanny accuracy. Truthfully, I don't think her shoe-size talent is as useful as my food-volume aptitude, but then again, she can play the piano and I can't.)

I worried that being considered an expert carried some heavy responsibility. For instance, what if someone asked me a technical question about dorky quilts, and I didn't know the answer? Should I just try to look intelligent and make something up? What if an interviewer asked: "Lisa, what is the origin of the Dorky Homemade Look?" I'd have to say, "Barbara Walters, that's a very interesting question!" (The guest is obligated to say this no matter how silly the question.)

Thinking fast, I'd say: "Interestingly enough, the first Dorky Homemade Quilt was invented in prehistoric times. The actual moment of creation went something like this:

"Urg turns to Moog while making her cave quilt and asks: 'Moog, what do you think of this purple fabric?'

"Moog replies: 'Urg, I think it's the ugliest fabric I've ever seen.'

"Urg: 'Hmmm . . . I think I'll use it anyway.'
"Thus, the 'Dorky Homemade Look' was born."

But what if Barbara Walters didn't believe me? She'd ask all those penetrating questions of hers—and find out that I can't play the piano.

If my husband was right, and I was now truly an "expert," I used to worry how the accompanying fame might change my life. In retrospect I can say that fame has changed my life in interesting ways. For example, I used to spend time in my shower, scrubbing my grout and thinking: "Here I am, Lisa Boyer, scrubbing my grout." NOW I say to myself: "Here I am, Lisa Boyer, expert at Dorky Homemade Quiltmaking, scrubbing my grout." As a matter of fact, in the first few days after my book was published, I narrated a lot of things that I did. "Here's Lisa Boyer, the famous Dorky Homemade Quilt Expert, grating a zucchini," or "Now Lisa Boyer, the Dorky Homemade Quilt Expert, is shampooing her hair." Imaginary applause would follow, which is pretty disconcerting when one is in the shower.

A year later I am now more comfortable with my status. Ellen didn't call, and no one ever asked me a single technical question. Believe it or not, it seems the quilting public is more interested in how to make non-dorky quilts than dorky ones.

Finally, you will be glad to hear that fame has not changed me all that much. This might be due to the fact that I didn't become all that famous, but that's okay. I've still got that plastic food-container thing to fall back on.

Tiara's Quilt

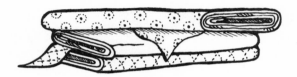

My son met his friend Tiara in preschool. They became friends shortly after he accidentally bopped her on the head with a red toy truck while playing in the sandbox one day. If you can bop a girl on the head with a truck and she still likes you, you've made a valuable friend for life, I always say. Tiara is a wonderful girl and a loyal friend to my son, and I am thankful for her presence in my son's life.

When Tiara and my son began the eighth grade together, I started planning in advance. I wanted to make my son's dearest friend a quilt for her eighth-grade graduation. Early in the year, I asked my son some leisurely questions, thinking that I had several months to make a quilt for Tiara. I asked him one morning to find out what her favorite color was. After a couple of weeks went by, he still hadn't told me what her favorite color was. "Maa-ahh-m! I can't just *ask* her!" he protested. Not wanting to embarrass or offend their 13-year-old sensibilities, I waited patiently for him to figure it out surreptitiously. After all, you can't ask a girl her favorite color. Horrors! What would she think?!

A few weeks later, I cornered him to find out what he discovered. "Hmmm . . . I know she hates purple," he said. "And don't make anything pink! Yellow is definitely out. Red may be okay, but I don't know. Not green. No brown."

So, armed with the idea that red, blue, or black may not be as highly offensive and objectionable as, oh, let's say, being seen with your parents at the mall, I went fabric-shopping. I found some adorable gecko fabric with none of the dreaded purple, pink, yellow, or brown. My idea was to make an attic-windows quilt with mischievous little geckoes peering in. There was a miniscule spot of forbidden green in the geckoes' eyes, but I was hoping that my son might not notice. But when I showed him the fabric he became apoplectic with horror. "Not GECKOES!!! She HATES geckoes! And don't get frogs either! Or unicorns or anything with rainbows—too babyish. And whatever you do, NO FLOWERS! And I thought I told you, no green!"

Thinking my son was being a bit dramatic and too opinionated, I cornered Tiara's mother and told her what I was planning. "What kind of things does she like?" I asked the 13-year-old girl's mother. She made a face. "Oh, that's a hard one. She doesn't like anything right now. Last week, she liked the color red and wore it every day, but she hasn't liked it for a couple of days now. She used to like pizza, but that was last week, and I'm sure it was just a phase. Oh, don't worry, I'm sure anything you make will be great."

I was beginning to think that I should have started this quilt right after the red-truck incident. Months had gone by, and all I knew was that Tiara, sweet girl that she is, seemed to dislike almost every color, creature, and plant on earth. Two months before graduation, I was desperately looking for something . . . anything . . . that a 13-year-old girl might not hate. I looked through books, scoured the Internet, and asked my friends' advice. No one could give me a clue about what a teenage girl might like. The list of what teenage girls didn't like, however, grew to monumental proportions. One friend, with an adolescent girl of her own, gave me the best advice. "Just make something, anything. She might not hate it . . . eventually."

Armed with that wildly inspirational advice, I gave up. I just closed my eyes and picked something. I picked fish. Colorful tropical fish set in pink, purple, and green squares. Fish in every hated color, fish swimming in and out of flowered borders, fish sometimes looking amazingly like geckoes and frogs. But I liked it, and eventually I hoped that she would.

I made the quilt top in a few days, as time had become short with all my indecision. When I was ready to quilt it, I asked my son for some meaningful words, phrases, and symbols to quilt into the top. I love to write secret messages in the quilting to be discovered later by the recipient. After a couple of hours of thought with a pencil and paper in hand, my son handed me a paper that was blank, except for the name of their school and the year. Instead of pressing him, I let him watch me quilt the name of the school and the year into Tiara's quilt. All of a sudden, he began thinking of some more words: "Red truck!" "Gizmo!" "Bean bag!" Finally, he got into the spirit of the thing, and we wrote all sorts of things into Tiara's quilt. I wasn't entirely sure that all of the words would mean anything to her, but he had fun anyway.

The last day of school, my son carried the quilt to school in a bag and presented it to his friend. She loved it and told us so. I guess we did all right after all.

A Perfect
Moment in Time

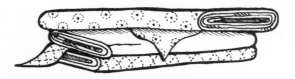

Now when I look back, I think it all must have started with Sandra Brigge's lunchbox. It was shiny pink vinyl and had pictures of dancing black circus poodles on it. The inside of the lunchbox had tiny zippered compartments for things like milk money and teeth that happened to fall out at school. The shoulder strap was long enough to pretend it was an oh-so-chic poodle purse, instead of a mere fourth-grade lunchbox.

Oh, how I loved Sandra Brigge's lunchbox. Every day at lunch, I would wait until Sandra was seated in the cafeteria. Then I would nonchalantly stroll by and just happen to pick a seat across and down from her. From my carefully selected vantage point, I could watch her unzip that box and take out her thermos and those pretty matching pink plastic food boxes. Her sandwiches were cut into perfect little crustless triangles; they were aligned carefully in the box along their diagonal edges. Her other pink boxes contained unbroken potato chips, fruit salad with teeny-tiny pastel marshmallows, and chocolate foam-filled cupcakes.

Meanwhile, I would look down at my paper-bag lunch with its crushed cotto salami sandwich on wheat bread, sadly oozing mustard and pale green lettuce out its crusty end. My sliced apple had gone brown hours before, and my chips were pulverized into salty granular dust. (Actually, it was my own fault; I never realized that the condition of my wretched lunch was the direct result of sitting atop it during the bus ride to school.)

It was at that moment in my fourth-grade brain, while staring down at my oozing salami sandwich, that I came to a shattering realization: there is more to an object than merely its function. My salami sandwich would fill my stomach, but there just wasn't any *art* in it. A pretty white sandwich would taste better. A pretty white triangle sandwich in a pink container would be delicious. And toss that pink container into a poodle lunchbox and that sandwich would become a gourmet delicacy!

Art had entered my life. From that point on, function took a back seat to form. Well, maybe not at that exact point, because in fourth grade I had no idea what that meant. But it did mean that the next morning, for the first time, I had a definite opinion about what I wanted to wear to school. I subsequently developed a distinct preference in hairstyles, much to my mother's dismay. (It was the mid-60s, but she was always trimming my bangs so that you could see my large and very white forehead in its embarrassing entirety. Since I had a billion freckles covering only the bottom half of my face, I looked like someone had taken a giant white paintbrush to my forehead. Honestly, I could have sold ad space up there.)

That same week, I decorated my bedroom. Half of my bedroom actually, because the other half belonged to my older sister, who didn't much care for my nine-year-old decorating flair. I don't remember alot about the color scheme, but I do remember looting my mother's costume jewelry and making my half of the room very sparkly. I clipped my mother's pins and earrings onto every surface, and my stuffed animals were adorned with her rhinestone chokers and tiaras. (Unfortunately, my mother didn't quite appreciate my artistry either, and Winky and Blue-Blue were unceremoniously stripped of their regalia later that same day.)

I suppose my family may have gotten used to having an artist in the family if it hadn't been for the night of the Paper Napkin Incident. My mother, who obviously was not an art-lover, used to buy only the plain white variety of paper dinner napkins. Day after day, year after year, we would wipe the barbecue sauce off our faces with plain, white, boring, colorless, unimaginative (did I mention white?), dinner napkins. The new-found artist in me saw a blank canvas. So before dinner one evening, I sat very patiently with my pens and painstakingly colored in all the embossed flowers on those stark white napkins. Oh, how beautiful they were. I used purples and greens and oranges and reds. Each napkin was a work of art; I had found my calling as an artist. I was going to fill the world with glorious color and beauty, one napkin at a time.

I set them on the table that night, and my family finally voiced their long overdue admiration for my artistic ability. It was my gallery debut, and I was the star. I was a little horrified when they each grabbed one of my works of art to use at dinner, but I realized that, as a true artist, I was expected to make sacrifices for my art. Dinner was served, and, as usual, the focus shifted to the pork chops and mashed potatoes.

A few minutes later, my sister looked up from her pile of peas. "Hey . . . Mom! Your face is green!" My mother looked up, and, sure enough, her face was green. And purple and orange and red. As sisters and brothers looked up from their meals one by one, I could see that they, too, were multicolored. My entire family's faces looked like a Van Gogh painting, replete with glorious multicolor swirls and flourishes.

Personally, I never thought my family looked more beautiful. They, on the other hand, held a unanimous opinion to the contrary.

To this day, I'm not quite certain about what was going through my nine-year-old brain when I used watercolor pens to decorate those napkins. Perhaps I had envisioned exactly the masterpiece I achieved: a perfect moment, frozen in time, of a confused multicolor family, dazed by the utter artistic genius of its youngest member.

Quilting in Hawaii

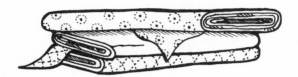

On a recent trip to southern California, I was invited to attend a quilting mini-group held at a home in Orange County. As I expected, the quilters there were a delightful group of women. We laughed, we told stories, and we shared our show-and-tell. At the time, I thought the meeting was very much like our quilt group meetings in Hawaii, except that these women were wearing a lot more clothing than we usually do, even in January. But things got very different from our get-togethers when the discussion turned to where the next meeting was to be held. For almost 30 minutes they discussed freeways, interchanges, routes, and diamond-lane information. Traffic was the major concern. "Take 60 over to 95 until you get to the 55 interchange; then you'll have to merge onto the 42. Don't take the 36 to the 44 because traffic is terrible after 2:00." And so on.

Traffic figures heavily into Orange-County quilters' lives. Unlike in many parts of the country, these women do not have to contend with severe weather conditions, so their quilting social life is much the same all year-round. They have an abundance of fabric shops, but traffic often determines which stores they frequent. The southern-California quilt guilds are commonly very large, boasting hundreds of members. Since the guilds are so big, they often meet at large public facilities, like community centers and church halls. A big parking lot is a must.

After visiting southern California, I began to wonder what factors affect quilting in other parts of the United States. I've often wondered how Alaskan quilters manage to meet in the winter, especially in sparsely populated areas. Do Texan quilters ever meet in non-air-conditioned houses? In densely populated areas like New York, how big are the quilt guilds? Do quilters in Seattle yearn for brightly colored quilts during their gray rainy spells? Some day I plan to see all these places and ask the quilters themselves: "What is quilting like where you live?"

So let me tell you what quilting is like where I live. I live in the state of Hawaii, on the tiny island of Kauai. Our island is vaguely roundish in shape and is only about 30 miles across. The center of our island is mountainous and inaccessible, so most of our population lives along the coasts. Even though we are a small island, we have varied climates on the different shores of our island. Our north shore has a moist climate and looks like a jungle. Our south and west shores are warm, dry, and desert-like. I live on the East Side, which is in between the two extremes. We get enough rain to keep our yard green all year long without the use of lawn sprinklers. Most of the year, the balmy tradewinds keep the heat and humidity at perfect levels.

We have only one major highway, which circles the island along the coast but does not make a complete circle. Imagine a horseshoe with the open end up. The far northwest shore, the Na Pali Coast, is inaccessible by automobile. This means that to go from the North Shore to the West Side, you have to go all the way around the bottom of the island to get there. Believe it or not, this can take up to three hours.

Having only one road affects our quilting social life. If you looked at our tiny island on the map, you might imagine that all the quilters on the island would know each other. But since we only have one highway, getting from one shore to another takes some time. For this reason, many quilters from the North Shore have never met quilters from the West Side, and vice versa. Ten miles is a long way to drive on Kauai. For this reason, we gather in small groups all over the island, instead of in one very large group.

The advantage to meeting in small groups is that we are able to meet in each other's homes. Some of our quilters have homes overlooking the ocean, while some of our members' homes are tucked away in the cool greenery of the upland areas. I love being invited to a quilting bee at a friend's cozy little plantation cottage, surrounded by a forest of banana trees and brightly colored ginger. Wild roosters run in and out of the greenery, crowing any time, night or day. And when the frequent rain falls upon the tin roof of the cottage, the noise is thrilling. A heavy rain will leave you shouting at the person standing next to you.

In the summertime, we often meet at June's house. June's home has a spectacular rock swimming pool perched over the cliffs at Kilauea. The edge of the pool looks like it spills right over the cliff and into the ocean. We bring our bathing suits and hold our friendship-group meeting in her pool. Show-and-Tell is difficult under these circumstances, but we manage.

Our gatherings usually feature a potluck lunch. Like in many guilds, salads and desserts are a favorite, all year long. Many of our dishes would be familiar to you, but would you recognize poi? Poi is a gooey paste made from the roots of the taro plant. It's sort of purple-gray in color, and it tastes somewhat like that glue kids got in trouble for eating in elementary school. (Uh-oh, I'm going to get mail about that comment!) Another dish you may not be familiar with is breadfruit—a giant, ugly fruit that looks like a green pincushion and tastes like a potato. Even though it's ugly (uh-oh, more mail), it tastes pretty good. Rice and sushi are popular potluck items, and, of course, anything with Spam in it. Pineapple, papaya, mango, cherimoya, star fruit, and bananas are always on the table, since most people grow these fruits in their yards. Dessert is usually chocolate; some things are universal.

After lunch we break out our newly completed quilts and unfinished projects. One thing that would strike you immediately about our quilts is that they tend to be very bright. I think this is because the world around us is so brightly colored. Hibiscus and ginger flowers are dazzling in shades of red, yellow, pink, and orange. Poinciana, plumeria, and shower trees litter the ground with color. The greenery is a brilliant green all year long. Even the local fish sport incredible purple, green, and yellow designs. Of course, the sky always lends a bright blue backdrop to the occasional white puffy clouds wandering across it, dropping a light rain as they pass. (Here, we call rain "Hawaiian Snow.") A gray or muted quilt would somehow look faded and sad next to all this color. And although it took me a full 10 years to use my first Hawaiian print in a quilt, I understand the appeal of those prints now.

Even though our quilts are made in Hawaii, they're not all Hawaiian quilts. An "Hawaiian quilt" is a term reserved for those beautiful snowflake-like, traditional, appliqué quilts which feature hand-quilting in an echo pattern. I made a single wallhanging of this style and, believe me, it was enough to make me appreciate the fine work and patience of the quilters within this tradition. A single Hawaiian quilt can take years to complete.

We are lucky to have four fabric shops on our island. Our fabric shops carry an incredible assortment of tropical and Hawaiian prints, not to mention a vast selection of batiks, which blend very well with tropical prints. If you're looking for brown or gray fabric, you'll have a hard time finding it on Kauai. Muted tones are a rare sight in our fabric shops. Reddish-brown fabric is definitely not a big seller here on our island; we have a collective dislike of anything that color.

Our dislike of reddish-brown has to do with our famous red dirt. Our soil on Kauai is a deep, rusty, reddish-brown substance that stains anything it comes in contact with. Shoes, clothing, paint, cars, feet, and children—are all stained reddish-brown. Frankly, we get sick of looking at it. So you won't find many brown quilts here; that is, unless they were once white—then you'll have no problem. They'll be on the clothesline next to my son's brown socks, which were also white . . . once.

Besides our red dirt, we deal with a humidity problem. Our scissors rust quickly and our stored textiles tend to mildew. (I have learned to consider mold a houseplant.) We never leave our hand-sewing needles "parked" in our projects, because they can rust within days. Sewing machines tend to have short, rusty life spans, as do cars and refrigerators. Disappearing fabric markers make marks that disappear almost immediately. I learned this after marking an entire quilt top one evening, and then waking up to an entirely blank quilt top the next day.

Of course, one of the loveliest things about living here is the weather. On Kauai, we are able to keep our windows open all year long. In the summer, the balmy trade winds keep us cool. In the winter, when the temperature can actually drop to 70 degrees in the daytime (brrrr!), we still don't close our windows. Winter is the time to bundle up, so many of us actually have to reach for our T-shirts with real sleeves. Shorts are comfortable all year long. Our feet are always bare, because shoes are left outside on the doorstep according to custom, no matter the weather.

Yes, the weather is lovely, but it isn't my favorite thing about living here on Kauai. My favorite thing about living here is the slow, relaxed way of life. I'll admit that when I first moved here from my native southern California, the slow pace drove me nuts. I suddenly had an abundance of time that I didn't have to spend in traffic, waiting in lines, or foraging for consumer goods. There were only a handful of stores and not many places I had to be. How was I ever going to keep myself entertained?

The answer, of course, was quilting. Kauai gave me the luxury of time. It took a couple of maddening years, but I finally adjusted to a slower way of life. For the first time in my quilting existence, I felt like I could sit still and hand-piece something. I could hand-quilt an entire quilt if I wanted to—what was the hurry? And when friends meet, we spend all day quilting, not just a few precious hours between obligations and/or traffic jams.

So there's your quick quilter's tour of Hawaii. My friends will let me know if I forgot anything. Oh yes, one more thing. I'm sure that they would want me to extend their fondest *alohas*, with an invitation to come visit the islands any time.

A hui hou!

About
the Author

Lisa Boyer became a
self-taught quilter at the
age of eight, patching
together a salesman's book
of bedspread swatches
with her toy sewing
machine. She only took a
few years off as she earned
her degree in microbiology,
worked as a clinical labora-
tory scientist, then became
a sewing-machine mechanic, pattern designer, quilt
teacher, writer, magazine columnist, and mother. Her
varied interests have led her to write articles on such
diverse topics as quilting, hurricanes, vegetables, shoes,
and sewing-machine repair, just to name a few.

Known to her friends as "the mad quilt scientist,"
Lisa combines her love of quilting with her background
in science and psychology, resulting in some strangely
unique philosophies. Her first book, *That Dorky
Homemade Look—Quilting Lessons from a Parallel*

Universe, was written as a tribute to all the lovely, but less-than-perfect, quilts and quilters everywhere.

Lisa's articles have appeared in *Kauai Magazine* and the *Orange County Register*, in addition to her regular column in *Quiltworks Today Magazine*. Lisa's quilts have appeared in *Quilting Today, Quiltworks Today, Miniature Quilts,* and *Kauai* magazines. She recently made a guest appearance on HGTV's "Simply Quilts."

Lisa Boyer is a native of southern California. She now lives in Hawaii on the island of Kauai with her husband, a clockmaker by avocation, and their son. Visit her on the web at www.lisaboyer.com.